Praise for
THE MILLIONAIRE MESSENGER

"We all have a life story and a message that can inspire others to live a better life or run a better business. Brendon Burchard's book proves it and shows how you can share your message to make a difference and also make an income. This book will help you change a lot of lives."

—Marci Shimoff, *New York Times* best-selling author of *Happy for No Reason* and *Chicken Soup for the Woman's Soul*

"The expert industry has been shrouded in myth and mystery for far too long. Now Brendon Burchard, one of our most innovative and powerful leaders, reveals exactly how we—authors, speakers, coaches, consultants, seminar leaders and online information marketers—make a difference and earn an income with our advice and expertise. This is an industry defined by how much value we add to others' lives, and this book delivers and shows exactly why Brendon is one of the best."

—Jack Canfield, *New York Times* best-selling author of *The Success Principles* and originator of the *Chicken Soup for the Soul*® series

"I love making a difference in the lives of millions of people worldwide. It gives my life a deep sense of meaning and purpose. I wish I had read Brendon Burchard's new book, *The Millionaire Messenger,* twenty years ago, because it has many of the lessons that would have dramatically boosted my career, both in terms of impact and finances. Lessons I had to learn the hard way. No matter what your age, now is the time to make the biggest difference in the world. Brendon will show you how."

—Daniel G. Amen, MD, *New York Times* best-selling author of *Change Your Brain, Change Your Life* and *Magnificent Mind at Any Age*

"This is a must-read for any author, speaker, coach, seminar leader, consultant, or online information marketer. Brendon Burchard shows you how to get your message to the public in a bigger way (and get paid for it, too)."

—John Gray, *New York Times* best-selling author of
Men Are from Mars, Women Are from Venus

"You were born to make a difference, to contribute and to share your gifts with the world. Brendon Burchard shows you how to make a living (maybe a fortune!) by making a positive difference in people's lives."

—Darren Hardy, Publisher of *SUCCESS* magazine and
best-selling author of *The Compound Effect*

"If you've ever dreamed of building a career and business around your advice, expertise and knowledge, then you'll love this book."

—David Bach, #1 *New York Times* best-selling author of
The Automatic Millionaire

THE
MILLIONAIRE
MESSENGER

Make a Difference and a Fortune
Sharing Your Advice

BRENDON BURCHARD

NEW YORK

THE MILLIONAIRE MESSENGER
Make a Difference and a Fortune
Sharing Your Advice

by BRENDON BURCHARD
© 2011 The Burchard Group LLC. All rights reserved.

ISBN 978-1-60037-938-3 (paperback)
ISBN 978-1-60037-939-0 (EPub)
Library of Congress Control Number: 2011922090

Published by:

an imprint of
MORGAN JAMES PUBLISHING
The Entrepreneurial Publisher
5 Penn Plaza, 23rd Floor
New York City, New York 10001
(212) 655-5470 Office
(516) 908-4496 Fax
www.MorganJamesPublishing.com

Interior Design by:
Bonnie Bushman
bbushman@bresnan.net

In an effort to support local communities, raise awareness and funds, Morgan James Publishing donates one percent of all book sales for the life of each book to Habitat for Humanity. Get involved today, visit
www.HelpHabitatForHumanity.org.

Also by Brendon Burchard:
Life's Golden Ticket
The Student Leadership Guide

Seminars by Brendon Burchard
Experts Academy
Partnership Seminar
High Performance Academy
World's Greatest Speaker Training
Empire Group Mastermind

Meet Brendon online and receive free training at
www.BrendonBurchard.com

DEDICATED to my dad, Mel Burchard, whose message to us kids throughout his life said everything you needed to know about the man and explains everything you need to know about me:

"Be yourself. Be honest. Do your best. Take care of your family. Treat people with respect. Be a good citizen. Follow your dreams."

CONTENTS

INTRODUCTION

This book builds three central arguments:

- Your life story, your knowledge, and your message—what you know from experience and want to share with the world—have greater importance and market value than you probably ever dreamed.
- You are here to make a difference in this world, and the best way to do that is to use your knowledge and experience (on any topic, in any industry) to help others succeed.
- You can get paid for sharing advice and how-to information that helps others succeed, and in the process you can build a *very lucrative* business and a profoundly meaningful life.

If any of this sounds unbelievable—especially the part about your getting *paid* for sharing what might essentially be your message to the world—then it is simply because you have been unaware of a fairly unknown and previously secretive industry that exists all around us—what I call the "expert industry."

The expert industry is a caring community of people who share their advice and knowledge with the world and get paid for it. These are the people you see on television and online sharing advice on how to improve your life or grow your business. They are ordinary people who have packaged their successes, research, or life story into advice for others and thus have become "experts" on a given topic, whether it is how to be a better parent, start a business, succeed at work, live with more passion, or any other topic. They are servants of wisdom, and they inspire all of us with what they know.

These experts, again, are just average people who have synthesized their life experience and have created products and programs for sale to the public. They have articles, blogs, books, audio programs, DVD home-study courses, podcasts, videos, and more, all of which are extremely easy and cheap to create thanks to the Internet. In many cases, they have become well known or famous simply for sharing their advice and how-to content. And they have made millions of dollars doing it. In effect, they have monetized their message, and they get paid more than you could ever fathom. They are millionaire messengers, the entrepreneurial experts of the Information Age.

Despite the fact that you may not currently consider yourself an expert or "guru," the fact is that anyone can be one. Don't worry; we will reframe the words "expert" and "guru" if you have a negative association with them, because being an expert or guru is just about helping people succeed, which is a very good thing. Becoming an expert is simply a matter of positioning and packaging *who you are* and *what you know* so that you can help the greatest number of people in your target audience. You can become a highly influential and highly paid expert on almost any topic you wish, and in this book I will show you how to do just that.

What I'm talking about is not about your becoming an expert in order to become a "knowledge worker" for some drone-creating global company. The knowledge worker is a long-dead concept, and in the new creative age—fueled by content, authenticity, trust, search engines, and social media—the new class of creatives and experts will work for themselves and create real relationships with people, based on valuable advice and information. Luckily, because of the great democratization of content and distribution that the Internet has brought us, every one of us can create and distribute valuable how-to content that helps other people. You are about to discover that in this new economy we can all be influencers, and we can all be paid for our knowledge without having to work for someone else. If you have a message and an Internet connection, you can have a career in the expert industry and get paid for what you know. It turns out that mentoring others can be both meaningful and profitable.

Importantly, this book is also not about making you a guru in the way most people have thought about it. It is not about telling you how you can become a "motivational" or "inspirational" speaker, though you can certainly do that, too. Traditionally, if you had an inspiring life story and wanted to make a difference in the world, everyone said, "Go be a motivational speaker." It is sad that our culture's only language to describe people who help others has traditionally been limited to the phrase "motivational speaker," when even those who operate under that moniker do so much more as experts. Speaking is just one of six areas an expert can be paid in; other areas include writing books, conducting workshops, coaching, consulting, and providing online training products and programs. Today's experts do not have to dominate in all these areas to become wildly wealthy. In fact, I will show you a million-dollar plan for getting your message out there and getting paid for it that may shock you in the simplicity of its implementation.

Having said all this, I have been wondering about something for a while. In the current fragile economy, when so many people are looking for their next step and desperately seeking advice, success strategies, and how-to information, how is it that no one has written a book like the one you now have in your hands? I believe this exact moment constitutes the greatest entrepreneurial opportunity in history and is a small part of a natural and logical development of our economy. People have a great need right now—they need guidance and mentoring and coaching—and you can serve them and make a massive difference (and a fortune) doing so.

I know that my words might sound surreal to you. So my aim in this book is to teach you about this industry and make these three arguments to you in such a concrete, rational, and implementable way that you take action and start inspiring and instructing others on how to succeed in life, business, relationships, or whatever topic you choose.

You can reach millions of people with your message, and you can get paid millions of dollars for doing so. I have proven it and so have my students. While it might sound like hype, keep reading and you might just discover a new career for yourself (and a higher calling).

On a personal note, I never knew about this industry, either, and I was always skeptical of anyone suggesting that you mix message and meaning with money and marketing. I did not, and still do not, like the word "guru," and I certainly never aimed to become one. Being from a small town, I had a general suspicion of "famous people." I grew up distrusting most "experts," and I never really thought about money, because we never had any.

So I can understand if this industry and my assertions might sound peculiar to you at first.

I didn't know I could get my message out there and help so many people and get paid at the same time. Frankly, I wouldn't have believed it if someone had told me.

But then I almost died. After that, I saw the industry for myself. And now I lead it.

This book is my effort to pull back the curtains and invite you in.

Chapter One

A CRASH COURSE IN SHARING MY MESSAGE

When I woke up, Kevin was screaming, "Get out of the car, Brendon! Get out of the car!"

I looked over from my seat on the passenger side of the car. Kevin was scrunched behind the wheel, screaming at me and trying to wrestle his way out of the smashed driver's side window. His entire face was covered in blood.

We had rounded the corner going 85 miles per hour. In the United States, that corner would have had a bright yellow sign with a U- shaped arrow, a warning sign indicating a sharp curve is coming up, so you'd better slow down.

But we were in the Dominican Republic on a newly paved road. No signs. And that corner was about to become a turning point in our lives.

It turned out to be a blessing. For months I had been depressed and emotionally dead following the breakup with the first woman I ever loved. I was only 19 years old, but I felt adrift, as if my life were over. We were high school sweethearts who had thought we might be married one day. But then we went to college together, and she discovered beer and boys. I didn't pay enough attention, and she cheated; it got ugly.

I was so upset that when an opportunity came to work a summertime job a world away in the Dominican Republic, I jumped at it. Getting out of town to escape my problems and depression was not enough—I had to leave the country.

So there I was in the Dominican Republic with Kevin, a friend from my hometown, helping out an entrepreneur we knew who sold trucking equipment. We were returning from a client's home around midnight. It was a dark, steamy Caribbean night. All the windows were down in our car, and John Cochran's "Life Is a Highway" was blaring on the radio. As we sped down the road, flanked by the dark jungle on either side, with the humid air funneling through the car, I felt a reprieve from my depression. The heaviness of my loneliness and sorrow diminished at the speed of sound. I closed my eyes, trying to forget that my soul felt dead, and I belted out that song at the top of my lungs.

Then Kevin screamed, "Jesus! Brendon, hold on!"

I opened my eyes and saw the headlight beams disappearing ahead of us, off the road into the darkness.

Kevin grabbed the wheel, cranking to the right, desperately trying to negotiate the turn. But it was too late. The car fishtailed, lost traction, and spun off the road. I braced myself and thought, "God, I am not ready." I did not feel I had fully lived my life yet. It's odd how real and lasting that feeling was. The slow-motion sense created by emergency was in full effect as we slid off the road. An urgent question went through my mind as we skidded into death's doorway: *Did I live?*

Careening off the road, our car smacked into a little retainer wall built for irrigation. We flipped into the air sideways, and I felt the seatbelt forcefully lock me into place. Then I felt a strange weightlessness as we were flipping…flipping.

My eyes were closed, but I saw them clearly. It was not like I thought it would be. I would have guessed I would see an omniscient viewpoint of my life, just like in the movies, where a reel of memories plays in slow motion, and you see yourself growing up. I didn't see myself now. No little Brendon running around at all.

But I see *them*. My friends and family are standing in front and to the side of me. They are singing around the cake on our living room table. It is my twelfth birthday party. My mom is crying happily and singing joyously that silly song she sings on our birthdays.

Then a different scene. It's my sister. She is swinging next to me on a swing set. Our eyes meet, and she smiles her big, beautiful smile.

Then more scenes. My life racing before me, experienced through my own eyes. All the scenes are moments when I am surrounded by those I love. I do not feel as if I were *in* the moments, though they look so real, and I am conscious that I am flipping through the air in slow motion. I think of those I love, and those who will miss me. A deep, powerful emotion of regret tugged at my mind: *Did I love?*

The car hit the ground with a body-rattling crash, and I was knocked out.

When I woke, I heard Kevin screaming to get out of the car. I looked over at him from my seat on the passenger side. He was scrunched behind the wheel, screaming at me and trying to get out of the car through the smashed window.

He turned to me, and I saw a gaping wound on the right side of his head, and his entire face was covered in blood. "Get out, Brendon!" he said with panic as he slithered through the window.

I didn't know if the car was on fire or what was happening. But Kevin's tone said enough. I looked to my right for escape but the passenger's side window frame was smashed. The whole roof and car was smashed down on top of me. My only escape was a narrow opening in front of me, what used to be the windshield.

I pulled myself through that space, cutting my arms and legs and the skin on my stomach, and I stood, somehow, atop the crumpled white hood of the car. I saw blood oozing from my body, over my feet and sandals, onto the top of the car. I felt dizzy, distant. Slowly, life was draining away and fear slid from my heart to my toes as I realized for the first time that life could really end. A weak and frightened energy then rushed through my body, and I wondered about the point of it all. I struggled through the thought and began to weep. *Did I even matter?*

A dark haze obscured my vision, and I felt I was going to pass out. *This is it,* I thought.

And then a shimmering sparkle at the end of the car's crumpled hood broke my trance. I saw a bright glint, a reflection of light, in my blood that was spilling off the side of the wrecked car. I looked up and saw a magnificent full moon in the darkness of the sky. It was a magical moon, something unlike any I had seen before—so close, so big and bright, so beautiful. I felt lifted from the wreckage of my life and deeply connected with the heavens and the waves of blue streaking across in the night sky. There was no pain, no feeling, a nothingness of silence for a moment that I will never forget. And then, slowly, a feeling of centeredness. I was not having an out-of-body experience; in fact, I had never felt more connected to who I was.

I felt a steadiness in my body, and a sense of gratitude washed over me, an appreciation for life that today I still cannot describe. It was as if, in that moment, I looked up to the sky and God had reached down, comforted me, and handed me life's golden ticket—a second chance at life. "Here you go, kid," the moment seemed to say. "You're still alive, you can love again, you can matter. Now, go on and get busy about it, because now you know the clock is ticking."

I remember looking into the sky that night, accepting that ticket, and thinking, "*Thank you. Thank you. I will earn this.*" A gratitude unlike anything I can describe entered my life, and it has never left. I felt tears run down my face—the good kind. And for the first time in months, my soul sang.

This is a story I have learned to share with more detail, presence, and heart each time I have told it to audiences from around the world.

Upon our return from the Dominican Republic—both Kevin and I survived, with our share of cuts and bruises and broken bones but alive and well, thank God—neither of us thought much about the accident.

That might seem odd, but I have learned that all of us discount our experiences in life and rarely seek to find and share their meaning.

In fact, when I returned to the United States and to college in Montana, I barely mentioned my accident except to close friends. I went on about life doing what you are supposed to do: Get a college degree, get some experience on a résumé, position yourself for a career, and take a good-paying job with a stable company.

But in the middle of the "supposed to do's," there was something deep within me that wanted to share what had happened. Some part of me was still connected to that moment, and I wanted to share "life's golden ticket" with others. I wanted to tell people that at the end of your life you are going to ask yourself three questions, because those questions changed me forever and set me on a path of passion and purpose.

At the end of your life you will want to know if you *really lived* your life fully—*your* life, too, not the hopes and dreams of your parents or teachers or peers or spouse. You will measure yourself to see if you were vibrant and cheerful and present and alive enough. You will want to know if you took enough risks and played hard enough, and dreamed big enough and fought valiantly enough to achieve your potential. You will want to know so much that it will ache in your bones, *Did I live?*

You will surely assess whether you cared enough and gave those around you enough attention and appreciation. You will ache to know who will miss you and whom you will miss. You will see an epic movie—at least, I did—of the times in your life when you were surrounded by love and friendship. You will question how open you were with your feelings, and your heart will demand, *Did I love?*

Finally, in your last moments, before the light has left you, a stirring deep in your body and in the forefront of your mind will wonder if there was a purpose to it all. You will question whether you lived a good life. You will want to know and sense and believe that you made a difference before you leave this world. Your soul will ask directly and loudly, *Did I matter?*

If any of this is true, I thought, if these are the three questions we will ask at the end of our lives, then I want to tell as many people as I can: *Why not live your life so that you are happy with the answers to these questions when the end does come?*

Why not live so fully and presently in every moment that you always feel alive and energized by the gift of life? Why not live through your heart and love with such intensity and frequency that the movie you see at the end of your life is a stirring love epic? Why not care for others and seek to make a difference in others' lives as part of your everyday schedule and routine, making it so ingrained in who you are that you *know* you mattered?

When I shared these three questions with a few friends, to my dismay, many seemed interested but not transformed. But a few of them found the questions profound and encouraged me to talk more about my story and accident.

The truth is, I was afraid to. Deep down, I wanted to shout all this from the rooftops. I wanted to focus people on what I thought was important. I dreamed about changing people's lives with this message, but when I awoke each morning I had no idea how to bring the dream into the daylight.

And there was all this work to do to get myself ready for a "real career" in the "real world." Besides, who would want to listen to some young punk kid talk about the meaning of life? Who would listen even if I knew how to get my message out there? Surely, I must be crazy.

Luckily, I stumbled upon a mentor, someone who also seemed passionate about life. At a very early and fortunate time in my life, I caught a glimpse of the "expert industry." And if I hadn't, surely my message would have died in my dreams.

Chapter Two

BEHIND THE GURU CURTAIN

Now you know a little about my story and my dream.

I just wanted to help people with what I knew about life, however limited it was for a guy at my youthful age. It was a deep stirring within to share a message with others. That is how it began for me: an experience I wanted to voice and share with others, but no understanding of *how* to go about doing so.

Perhaps you can relate. Maybe you have learned something about life or about business that you would like to share with others. You already know that mentoring others is a path to a meaningful life. A stirring within you to share your voice and your knowledge and your life's lessons is within you. But how can you make a real impact when you have to work so hard just to make a living? How can you get your message out there and really influence others in a deep and meaningful way?

For months after returning from the Dominican Republic, I lay awake in my tiny dorm room wondering about these questions. Then one night a messenger came to me and awoke something in me that transformed my life. That messenger, oddly, was a man on television. He was not a preacher or televangelist, though he sounded at times as passionate and directive. He was a larger-than-life character who spoke a language about life that I seemed to understand. His name was Tony Robbins, and he had a message: You have unlimited personal power to live the life you desire and make a difference, and I can help you tap into it.

I want to tell you right now that I know all this might sound silly. I am as distrustful of television and infomercial "stars" as anyone else. But this guy won me over. It was not just what he was saying; it was what he was *displaying*—he was helping people with what he knew about life, and

I wanted to do the same thing in some way. That night I bought his audio program, called "Personal Power II," and because I wanted quick help, I paid for fast shipping. It was the second purchase I ever made on a credit card. I listened to that program over and over, often when I was going home from college on a three-hour drive over the Rocky Mountains. The concepts in the program were stunning for a young person to hear: You control your destiny, step up, make a new decision for yourself, let your values guide you, live with passion. I can say without hesitation that the program dramatically changed my life.

In the years that followed, I listened to and read similar messages from the self-help and business world gurus—from Wayne Dyer and Deepak Chopra to Stephen Covey and David Bach, to John Gray and John Maxwell. Most of these life and business experts had books, tapes, CDs, DVDs, seminars, and coaching programs that they sold to the public. I bought many of them and consistently did anything I could to improve my life and do well in my career and relationships. I was living a good life, guided by my three questions and the wisdom of those who were sharing their message with the masses.

I suppose this is a common story, as these experts have helped literally tens of millions of people around the world improve their lives. *But here is where I am different and where your story and mine now intersect.*

The difference that brought me to this day and writing this book is this: When I listened to these leaders' voices I always thought, "Why can't *I* be that voice of inspiration and instruction for people someday? How are these men and women getting their message out there, helping people and building real businesses doing it?"

It was those questions that played in my mind as I left college and entered the real world as a different kind of "expert," an organizational consultant. For about seven years I worked for a global consulting company. I enjoyed it and advanced easily but did not find that work to be my life's work.

While collaborating with clients, I would often share my car accident story, and I started to notice that people were really connecting with me and my message the older I got. They would say, "Man, you have to tell that story to people! You should get your message out there." I would ask how and they would say, "Well, the only way to get your message out there is to write a book, or give a speech, or do a workshop, or put up a website, or be a life coach or something like that."

Everyone seemed to say the same thing—become an author, speaker, coach, seminar leader, consultant, online advice guru—but no one knew *how* to do that. You certainly do not go to school for that, right? When I looked on the Internet for advice on how to get my message out there, all I found was a hodgepodge of information on how to write a book, get on television, or make money as a motivational speaker. But no one was talking about how to have a real, sustainable career helping people with valuable how-to information.

Ultimately, the stirring in me to share the story of my accident was so profound and urgent that I left my cushy corporate job. I decided to jump wholeheartedly (and perhaps foolhardily) into what I then narrowly labeled "the guru industry." I was committed to sharing my message and figuring it out on my own, with or without any training or credentials for doing so.

Within a year, I followed in the footsteps of those who had come before me, those who had left a real job to go out and follow their dreams and share their important message with the world. And I got the same results as most of them: I promptly went broke.

The sad truth about this world is that it is *not* set up to help people share their real voice and their real message. We are a society that does not adequately value mentorship or sharing life experience and lessons with others, so there is no "career path" for doing so. Tragically, in our culture, helping other people with what we know is seen as a nice end-of-life activity best done between golf and sitting on the beach while living large off our 401(k)s.

With no training and without a clue about how to share and profit from my advice and my how-to information for living a meaningful life, I fell into frustration and financial woes. I embodied the cliché of the poor, struggling writer, and I dug deeper and deeper holes of debt as I bought every book, audio program, and seminar ticket I could on the topics of becoming an author, speaker, coach, consultant, seminar leader, and online information marketer (i.e., someone who sells their advice, training, and information on the Web).

Nothing was working, and by the end of my first year, I was turned down by dozens of publishers for what I felt was my life's message distilled into a parable: a novel about second chances, called *Life's Golden Ticket.*

My story was unfortunately, the story of millions of people: We want to get our message out there but have no idea how.

But if there is one thing you should know about me, it's that when I have a vision for something I have no problem dedicating myself to learning the *how* of making it happen. I am a tireless and determined student and researcher, and I never let my dreams die in the daylight.

So I immersed myself even more deeply into this odd world of becoming an expert. It was a lonely, frustrating, and expensive quest. I started combining everything I learned from all the disparate sources I could. I would pull information I learned from a writers' conference, spin it with something I learned at a seminar for public speakers, add something I learned about Internet marketing, incorporate something I learned at a life-coaching association meeting, and then mix it all up with what I saw the big-name gurus in multiple industries and topics doing online and offline. If no one had connected the dots out there and thought of this as a real career in a real industry, then I would be the first.

In the following year, just 24 months after deciding to jump into the "expert industry," I started seeing *massive* results. Now, this is the part where I share my results with you. I do so not to impress you but rather to show you how fast things can change when you finally crack the code on positioning, packaging, and promoting your message intelligently and strategically in the marketplace.

In those wild and joyful two years, I reached millions of people with my message and made over $4.6 million inspiring and instructing people on how to improve their lives and share their own message.

Within three years, I became a best-selling author (*Life's Golden Ticket* was published by HarperCollins in 2007), a $25,000-per-speech keynote speaker, a seminar leader who sells out every event (some at $10,000 per ticket), a life coach, a small business consultant with a multiyear waiting list, and an online information marketer who averaged around $2 million for every major promotion I put online. I did this all working from home and without a single full-time employee—I had only a small team of contractors brought in on a project-by-project basis.

In that same time period, I shared the stage with the Dalai Lama, Sir Richard Branson, Stephen Covey, Deepak Chopra, John Gray, David Bach, Jack Canfield, Debbie Ford, Brian Tracy, Keith Ferrazzi, T. Harv Eker, Paula Abdul—and the list goes on and on. I created articles, videos, audio programs, DVD home study systems, and online training programs that have helped tens of thousands of people completely transform their lives and businesses. Global nonprofits and Fortune 500 companies started sponsoring my message, and now I couldn't contain my message even if I wanted to.

This all sounds too incredible, I know. For many it sounds out of reach. But you will soon discover that not only is it possible—and possible without a lot of resources or any employees whatever—but there is also a replicable system for starting all this. In coming chapters, I will share with you success stories from others who have achieved impressive results and helped thousands of people, and I will show you how it all adds up to millions of dollars fairly quickly.

I succeeded so much in this expert space that people began asking me, "Brendon, how did you do all this so fast? How in the world do you get a book out there, or get hired as a speaker, or do your own workshops, or become a life or business coach, or launch your programs online?"

Soon, I was so inundated with requests that I decided to create a training program for people starting out just as I had done. Twenty-seven people showed up to the first training. Today, thousands of people from around the globe travel to Experts Academy, the only comprehensive training program in the world for authors, speakers, coaches, consultants, seminar leaders, and online information marketers. To my amazement and deep appreciation, the marketplace and expert community celebrated the arrival of Experts Academy. For the first time ever, someone had connected the dots and approached the guru space as a real career in a real, legitimate service-based industry.

My story came full circle in 2009. From those sleepless nights in college hoping to share my story and message with others to now being recognized as a leader in the expert community, I had come a long way.

I was soon asked to mentor my mentor and give back. In 2009, I was honored to step onto Tony Robbins's stage and inspire his audience of more than 2,000 gathered in the Meadowlands. I also welcomed Tony onto my stage at Experts Academy. The student and his teacher had met each other and, together, helped thousands of people.

As of this writing, Tony and many of the top self-help, relationship, and business experts in the world have all become my dear and trusted friends. Many have also become my clients, and many have also stepped onto the stage at Experts Academy to reveal, for the first time in their careers, exactly how they found and shared their message as well as built their businesses.

All I ever wanted to do was share my message. Now I am known as "an expert at helping people become experts," and to my surprise and with much humility, I have become the de facto leader and spokesperson for the "expert industry."

I share all this backstory because I want you to know that I have been where you are now. I have struggled to get my message out there, too, but now I am here to help you. I have trained thousands of people just like you on how to make a difference—and a fortune—with their advice, experience, and knowledge. You'd recognize many of my client and alumni names—they are talk show hosts, radio personalities, well-known national and international celebrities, *New York Times* best-selling authors, famous speakers, elite online marketers, highly paid consultants, and national spokespersons. You have seen my students on *Dr. Phil, Oprah, Rachael Ray, CNN, Fox News,* and *YouTube* as well as in the *Wall Street Journal, New York Times, USA Today, Success* magazine, and pretty much every major media outlet in the world.

What I am even more proud of is all the experts I have trained whom you may never have heard of—people out there right now sharing their advice and helping others succeed in hundreds of areas. Alumni and up-and-coming experts from my events are helping children succeed in school, women find jobs, baby boomers ready themselves for the next stage of their lives, new couples buy houses, loved ones deal with death and grief, doctors care better for their customers, obese people rediscover healthy lifestyles, small-business owners do better marketing, professionals pass their certification exams, speakers learn how to own the stage better, wine lovers pick better wines, veterans start new careers—and the list goes on.

What is possible for you and your message—if you haven't found it yet, don't worry, I'll help—is likely beyond your imagination right now. That's because very few people have ever been exposed to the expert industry, and most people don't understand the world of the entrepreneurial expert. It is a new career choice for many and a very different way of thinking about work.

In the next chapter I will begin pulling the curtains back on our lifestyle, and then, in the following chapter, I'll show you how you can join us. It's your time. All you have to do is decide if this is the right calling and opportunity for you. Let's get started.

Chapter Three

THE EXPERT CALLING
AND LIFESTYLE

In the coming chapters I will reveal how experts start out and exactly how they get their message out to the world (and how they get paid for it). I will also address the number one objection I know you have right now: "Gosh, Brendon, I'm not an expert, and who would pay me anything for what I know?"

Don't worry; we'll get to your childhood fears of inadequacy soon enough. (Just kidding.) We will address this concern, because most people tragically undervalue what they know, or have never actually thought about what they know and how valuable it could be for others.

But before we get to your specific expertise, I want to paint a picture of the broader expert industry so that you can determine if you even want to be a part of it. Trust me, you can become a highly paid expert in any field and on any topic, which I will prove to you in coming chapters. For now, we should discuss whether this is really a calling and career you are interested in.

Yes, I believe becoming a Millionaire Messenger is a calling and a real career. It is a calling because I deeply believe it is part of our life's purpose to learn and experience the world and then turn and lend a hand to others who are also trying to get ahead. If you have struggled through something and survived, you should help those now struggling. If you have achieved the impossible, make it possible for others to achieve the same. If you have spent years figuring something out, why not shorten someone else's learning curve? If you have cracked the code to success in any area, why not give *everyone* the secret?

Obviously, all this has a "help others" bent to it, and for that I am often criticized. Some in our community have called me a bleeding heart and a "softie" because I often focus more on the mission than on the money. But I believe that coming from a place of service is not only a strong spiritual practice but also good business. If you care about helping others, then they will believe in you—and, yes, they will buy from you.

I believe everyone has a message and a life story or experience that can help other people. You have a message, too, even if it is yet undefined. You have something in you that you have been told to deliver to the world: your unique voice and contribution. You have been called to deliver it, and this book will help with that.

In terms of a career, there are few more stable and lucrative jobs in the world than that of being an "expert." People will always need help and advice in their personal and professional lives. Every generation needs parenting advice, real estate advice, marketing advice, relationship advice, business advice, love advice, financial advice, career advice, technology advice, spiritual advice, and so on. There is no limit to how many people search for and need your knowledge and information.

This point has been proved by the enduring and powerfully influential careers of our industry's leaders and legends. When an expert finds his or her real message and delivers it with care, compassion, and consistency, the world takes note. Consider the often-told stories of these experts:

> Tony Robbins has been inspiring people to find their personal power for over 30 years, and he has reached millions of people worldwide and built a $50,000,000 empire under his brand in the process.

> Stephen Covey took seven simple habits for being effective and built a billion-dollar training company while keeping *The Seven Habits of Highly Effective People* on the business best-seller list for over *twenty-one years*.

> Zig Ziglar has given essentially the same success speech for almost 40 years, and he still turns down business all the time.

> Rick Warren turned his spiritual advice into the best-selling hardcover nonfiction book of all time, *The Purpose Driven Life*, with over 30 million copies sold. He built a 20,000-member congregation in California, and in 2008 he hosted the Civil Forum on the Presidency, featuring presidential candidates Barack Obama and John McCain.

David Bach started giving financial advice to the public after leaving his corporate job in the financial sector and turned it into the number one financial advice brand in the world, with a slew of *New York Times* best-selling books including *Start Late, Finish Rich* and *The Automatic Millionaire*. Major corporations have sponsored his message and helped him reach millions of people (and make millions of dollars). He is on *The Today Show* all the time. Suze Orman, Jim Cramer, and Dave Ramsey are other well-known and enduring names in the financial advice area.

Wayne Dyer, Ph.D., traded his academic career for an advice career and became an internationally renowned author and speaker in the field of self-development. He's the author of over 30 books, has created many audio programs and videos, and has appeared on thousands of television and radio shows. He has had a bestselling book every decade for five decades in row. His books *Manifest Your Destiny, Wisdom of the Ages, There's a Spiritual Solution to Every Problem*, and the *New York Times* bestsellers *10 Secrets for Success and Inner Peace, The Power of Intention, Inspiration, Change Your Thoughts—Change Your Life*, and *Excuses Begone* have all been featured as National Public Television specials.

John Gray took a simple idea, that men and women often seem to be from different planets, and turned it into a three-decade phenomenon of books, speeches, workshops, coaching, and online videos under the *Men Are from Mars, Women Are from Venus* empire.

Oprah and her friends and contemporaries have dominated television and books for decades, from Rachael Ray on cooking advice, to Dr. Phil on life and relationship advice, to Marianne Williamson on spiritual advice, to Bob Greene on exercise advice, to Tim Gunn on fashion advice, to Nate Berkus on home and garden advice, to Dr. Mehmet Oz on health advice.

Of course, many of these people are now household names, and many are now best-selling authors and celebrities on television. I mention them here because they have name recognition and can give a "face" to the expert industry. They also illustrate the diversity of expertise that they have all mastered and monetized: from personal development to personal finance, from relationships to lifestyle design, from business to spirituality.

What is important to know about these examples is that none of these people started out rich and famous. They started out just like you. What they did next was build their expertise, learn to package and promote their message, and figure out a way to serve as many people as they could.

You do not have to aspire to be a celebrity expert. Maybe that is not your thing. Personally, I have avoided traditional media up until recently, when I felt that a new style and new leadership were required in the industry.

I have seen and met tens of thousands of other experts who enjoy a meaningful and abundant life in the expert community and are not famous. You might not know their names, but their work is helping thousands of people through their how-to information and products. They have real careers, and they make real money. They are on stages across the country, they're doling out advice online, they're training companies in your local business loop, and they have books, CDs, DVDs, and training materials galore. If you ever attend my Experts Academy seminar, you will meet hundreds of everyday people doing this successfully and happily, many on topics you never imagined someone could be a successful expert in.

I love the story of Lorie Marrero. Lorie had a passion for organizing her and her friends' homes. People would go to her house and say, "Lorie, how in the world do you keep everything so organized?" Unlike most people, Lorie is a fantastic listener and unconsciously understood that if a lot of people ask you about something, *ding,* there's business there as an expert. So Lorie started positioning herself as an organizing expert and started coaching people and organizations on how to better organize their homes and workplaces. Yes, she became an expert organizer. She created an online program on her topic and eventually wrote a best-selling book, *The Clutter Diet: The Skinny on Organizing Your Home and Taking Control of Your Life.* Lorie is now the national spokesperson for Goodwill Industries International and is the ambassador of Goodwill's Donate Movement. She has also done spokesperson work for companies, including Staples and Microsoft. She is a frequently sought-after expert for national media, including *Good Housekeeping,* CNBC, and *Woman's Day.* The Container Store and other retailers carry Lorie's products nationwide.

Now, here's a question: Have you ever heard of Lorie? Many have not. Many of you reading this book never heard of me, either. You see, there are tens of thousands of us out there, and often people don't discover us until they have a problem they need fixed. Can't organize your life? You find Lorie. Can't get your message out there, you stumble onto Brendon. This is the way of the nonfamous expert world—as has been said, when the student is ready the teacher will appear.

Here's another story. Marci Shimoff was a woman who was, simply, happy. People were always asking her, "Marci, why are you so happy?" Her reply was, "No reason not to be." Just like Lorie, Marci listened to people and started speaking, coaching, and writing on the subject of happiness. She eventually became a *New York Times* best-selling author. Her book title? *Happy for No Reason.*

Lorie's and Marci's stories not only illustrate that anyone can become an expert on any topic but also provide an important lesson. The best way to find your area of expertise is to ask yourself, "What is it that people are always asking me how I do?" or "What are the questions people always seem to be asking when they deal with the subject of _____?" Answer those questions and serve others, and you have an expert business.

How about Roger Love? Ever heard of him? I hadn't until I started looking for an expert to help me with my voice. I started losing my voice during my four-day seminars, and I was scared my career was over. My friend Tony Robbins mentioned Roger to me, and I then discovered an expert in an area of expertise I had never even heard of. Roger turns out to be the number one vocal coach in the world. He does coaching, speaking, and training, and he has a slew of fantastic books and CDs on vocal performance. I would never have heard of him, but he has coached some folks you may have heard of, including John Mayer, Reese Witherspoon, Tyra Banks, Maroon 5, Eminem, and many of the top actors and singers in the world.

Rick Frishman was a retiree from the world of public relations. When he decided to have a second career and reflected on his first, he realized his favorite clients from the PR world had always been book authors. So he began a second career as an expert on book publicity and publishing, and he created a series of books and workshops called Author 101 to help new authors succeed. He made a fortune in the process, but more importantly, he helped thousands of authors learn how to get their message out there through our most honored medium: the art of writing.

Frank Kern was a dog trainer from Macon, Georgia. One day he discovered how to sell dog training advice online and started to make some good money doing that. Soon people were asking, "Frank, how do you do that online information marketing?" Thus was born his career as an Internet marketing expert. Today, Frank is the highest-paid Internet marketing strategist in the world, and his online promotions regularly bring in $6 million for his clients. He also helped craft one of the largest Internet marketing campaigns, which made more than $20 million in a few weeks.

Shane and Chantal Valentine were everyday parents with a beautiful baby named Alina. They were also both foodies, and they wanted Alina to grow up eating healthy, fresh food instead of that muck that comes in jars. So they started cooking fresh organic baby food for Alina, spoiling her with great cuisine from around the world. Soon people were asking, "Hey, how do you cook all those great baby food recipes?" Thus was born their new career as "baby cuisine experts." Since then, they've created healthy cuisine programs and promotions with Clif Bar, Pixar Studios, and Whole Foods. Who would have imagined they could have become experts in baby cuisine?

I could literally share *thousands* of stories of everyday people like Lorie, Marci, Roger, Rick, Frank, and Shane and Chantal who have become successful and highly influential experts on every imaginable topic. I meet them all year long through my Experts Academy events.

But this is a book about *you,* so I am going to spend less time on inspirational stories and more time on instructing you personally. If you want to meet hundreds of people in this industry, just join us at Experts Academy someday. From here forward, this book is about *you.*

Let's now get to the work of deciding if this is a community *you* really want to be part of. Here are nine reasons I think the "expert industry" is the finest industry in the world to have a career in.

1. Your work is based entirely on your passion and knowledge.

The expert industry is, without doubt, one of the most passionate and energetic industries in the world. Just come to one of our seminars and you will see that this is true. Why? Because ours is one of the few industries, aside from the music industry, that is founded on its members' finding and sharing their unique voice with the world. It turns out that *sharing* and *teaching* is a true art that ignites a deep well of passion within the human spirit. This passion is one reason so many fans and followers are inspired by experts—they are attracted to the energy and zest for life and business that experts show the world.

But this does not mean our industry is based solely on a wild and exuberant "rah-rah" energy. Our passion is matched and grounded by wisdom and intelligence. The truth is, you can't succeed in our industry unless you have knowledge that can help other people overcome their challenges or move from point A to point B.

So here are the essential interview questions I would ask anyone seeking a career in the expert industry: Are you deeply passionate about your topic and about inspiring other people to improve? What knowledge do you have about life or business that could help other people?

2. Your work activities center on "relating and creating."

How do most people spend their workdays in the "real world"? How would you describe their two principal work activities?

In the expert community, we spend our time on only two things:

- *Relating* with our audience to gain their trust and understand their needs and ambitions, and
- *Creating* useful information, content, and products that add value to our audience and teach them how to live a better life or grow their businesses.

That is pretty much our entire job.

Even our sales and marketing is really just relating with our customers— giving them value and sharing information with them through our websites, blogs, articles, products, and videos. Despite the old myths, you don't have to be a sales genius, an over-the-top charismatic, or a snake-oil salesman to succeed in our industry. The reality is that we are seeing a massive influx of new members in our community precisely because more and more people are seeing that sharing their message can be done in this new era of marketing without "pushing" others to believe in us. People are seeing that our sales are, in fact, very "soft" and service-driven. I can say with authority that across topics and niches, it is readily apparent that all of our industry's sales campaigns that are working essentially run like this: We send out free information that adds value to people's lives, and then at some point we say, "Hey, if you liked that free information, I also have a product/program that you can buy, which goes much deeper." How easy is that?

To win, we experts just have to know our customers well. We need to have compassion for those struggling with certain challenges, and we need to create a map for them to follow to improve their situation, whether at home or at work. It's a real relationship business. The better we know our customers and what they need, the more we can tailor our messages and methods to help them.

Once we know our customers, our job is in creating unique and valuable how-to information for them. I typically call this "packaging your information," meaning creating helpful articles, webinars, videos, audios, workshops, coaching programs, and so forth that deliver your message. The creation part of this business is what I believe activates the most energy and artistic expression in our work. You'll often hear people at my seminars screaming with joy, "I am a creator!" as they realize they can once again tap into the creative and expressive part of their lives that was cut off in their "real world" work.

Because our work is so focused on creating and relating, I like to say that the expert community is truly the first real landing place for what Richard Florida termed "the creative class." Most creatives around the world wish they could create more things, especially idea-driven concepts that help people live better lives. Well, that's what we do, full-time. Experts are the most idea-driven and content-creating segment of the economy, period. We live in the information world, and we are creating it all. We are the artists and the drivers of the Information Age.

3.   You work anywhere and anytime, starting now.

When Tim Ferriss wrote *The 4-Hour Workweek,* he had no idea how big it would get or how many people would find his approach completely unimaginable. But of course it was easy for Tim to imagine a four-hour workweek: He's an expert. Armed with only a laptop and phone, most experts can make millions of dollars working anywhere they want and anytime they want.

I know this to be true. When I began, all I had were those two gadgets. I had no money, no influence, no name recognition, no rich uncle, nothing. I was armed with only a message and a dream, and soon my computer became my only needed resource. My laptop became my ATM, allowing me to write articles and books and create and post webinars, videos, and online programs that people paid me for. My phone allowed me to do "teleseminars," or group conference calls that people pay to join. I did 100 percent of this from home. Today, while running five million-dollar brands in the expert industry, I still work mostly from home or at Experts Studio, a condo where I set up a video studio. The cost of a nice video studio setup today is less than $2,000.

Very few start-up opportunities in the world, aside from Internet-based businesses, require so little in capital investment or resources. Based on my experience in the expert space and our alumni surveys from Experts Academy, I have previously estimated that 92 percent of our industry works from home. We often say, "Message? Check. Knowledge? Check. Audience to serve? Check. Laptop and phone? *Expect* checks."

4. You work with whom you want.

As entrepreneurs, experts hire and fire anyone they want, and that can include letting go of rude customers. We are not at the mercy of horrible bosses, weird coworkers, corporate kiss-ups, or any other ladder climber who plays office politics. Because it's an industry based solely on our individual passion, our knowledge, and our ability to relate to our audience and create valuable information for them, we control our own fate. We are entrepreneurial experts, and all the benefits of being an entrepreneur thus apply.

But the benefit of being in the expert community is not just that we don't have to work with unpleasant sorts. It is also that we can choose whom we *do* work with. Those in the expert space are incredibly open to collaborations, joint ventures, content sharing, and promotional partnerships. Because we all know that our first mission is to share our message, we will take almost any opportunity to share our message, whether it's being interviewed by each other or being featured in each other's books or product packages.

I'll give you an example. Tony Robbins was working on creating a new course he called "The New Money Masters." He wanted to interview people who had really mastered online information marketing. Now, he could easily create that program himself, but knowing that this is a creative and collaborative community, he chose to interview other experts. Tony asked me to participate, and I happily agreed. I flew out to his video studio the very next day, and we shot a great interview. I was not paid for it and didn't ask to be paid for it, because I know that sharing my message is job number one and because in this community it's great to collaborate. In all, Tony interviewed twelve of the best-of-the-best in the online marketing space, including my friends Frank Kern, Eben Pagan, John Reese, Dean Jackson, Jeff Walker, and Mike Koenigs—the man who introduced many of us to Tony. The course went on to be a multimillion-dollar smash. I have appeared in two other formats for Tony, and he returned the favor by speaking at and promoting my Experts Academy seminar.

I share this example because it illustrates several points. First, experts are always open to sharing their expertise to get their message out there. Imagine the reality that you can work alongside your mentors and gurus. It is profoundly empowering.

Second, because of the collaborative nature of the industry, *you* don't have to be the guru on every topic—you can just interview other experts. You see, I can't be or teach what Tony Robbins teaches, so I bring him in to teach my people his stuff, and he does the same with me. If I want to bring in an expert on any topic into my events or feature their advice on my websites or webinars, those experts are only an e-mail away. Experts are incredibly open and accessible people. This surprises newcomers all the time.

Finally, it shows that if you make a real difference, as Tony has since day one, then others will support you and help you out. I love that about this community.

I have been blessed to work with everyone I ever dreamed of working with in the industry so far. My work has helped me meet presidents, spiritual leaders, celebrities, CEOs, and pioneers in almost every industry I have ever been curious about. The reality that experts are so open to sharing their expertise is one of the greatest benefits of what we do. Later in this book, I will candidly discuss how we need to get better about sharing insights on our *businesses,* not just our content areas of expertise.

5.   Your promotions are based on your promotions.

I love this truism: As an expert, if you want to be paid more, you simply promote more (assuming, of course, you do a good job at it).

Unlike the organizational pay-me-by-the-hour world, your pay promotions are not based on an uncontrollable thumbs-up from your manager. Instead, your pay is based on how much you are doing to promote your message and information products and programs to the world. In general, the more promotions you do well, the more revenue you make and the more people you serve. That is why I am always saying you can make a difference *and* a fortune simply by promoting good advice and how-to information.

This concept becomes more and more powerful as you gain more and more fans and followers. The bigger your audience, the bigger your revenues will be, assuming you are adding value, creating a deep and real relationship, and selling strategically and intelligently. These are all things we teach at Experts Academy.

But don't worry, your pay is not based solely on the size of your subscriber list, as many newbies fear. We *all* started with no list, no fan base, no outlet for our voices. But we built more and more of a following the more value we added.

The fearful emotions that come up from the reality of having a small list can be assuaged by my last point: You can work with others in the expert community. Never forget that *other* experts and outlets, like the media, have big audiences, and they can help you get your message out there. For example, you can be interviewed and promoted by other experts in your genre and share in any profits made. I will cover this concept, called *affiliate marketing,* later.

Let's look at this overall concept in motion. Every time I put together a promotion these days, I can usually make $200,000 with a few e-mails. The more e-mails I send, the more I make. Naturally, I have to make sure I don't sell too much to my audience, but you get the point. And the smarter my promotions and the more I engage others to promote with me, the more people I can reach with my message and the more money I can make. Recently, I launched a new training program and made over $2 million in just 10 days. That was a nice promotion.

As I shared before, you don't have to be intimidated by all this talk of promotions and marketing. As I said, all of our sales campaigns essentially work like this: We send out free information that adds value to people's lives, and then at some point we say, "Hey, if you liked that free information, I also have a product/program that you can buy, which goes much deeper." That is a very empowering thing to know, and that is exactly how I recently made that $2 million. Now I know that anytime I want to earn more income, I just have to add more value to the marketplace and then offer a related sale.

I know that some people don't like my sharing financial numbers and talking about money, but I think it's important. I think the larger culture needs to know that meaning and money can mix and that as you make more money you can help more people, and vice versa.

6. Your pay equals the value you deliver, not the hours you work.

Hourly work is a horrible reality for most people. But hourly work is not for well-trained experts. We are not paid by the hour for our worth—how do you charge for the invoice item "changed my life in an hour"?—but by the value we give. It can take a tremendous amount of time for people from the corporate or traditional work world to understand this fact. It sure took a long time for me.

I remember, when I was first starting out, getting a phone call from a man who had heard about my message. He asked me if I would be his life coach and help him think through his life and plan for something greater. He was fifty-three, and at the time I was about half his age. We spoke for a while, and he seemed to lack clarity about who he was and where he wanted to go in life. I asked him a few questions that he felt were profound and helpful. At the end of the call, he asked how much I charged. I hadn't really thought about it before, and sheepishly I told him I had never been a life coach or worked one-on-one with people—I had instead been a consultant to companies, and an author of books.

Since I didn't know how to answer his question about pricing, I asked, "Well, based on what you're trying to do, how much do you think I should charge?"

He quickly replied, "Well, I hear that life coaches get paid two hundred dollars an hour. Let's start there."

At that point I almost fell out of my chair. I thought, *Two hundred an hour! That's what a good lawyer gets paid!* Then I said, "Sure." That was a lot of money to me at the time.

Within months, everything was going so well that other people started asking me to coach them. And in that amount of time, I heard about other life and business coaches who were charging between $300 and $1,000 per hour. So I raised my fees to $600 an hour and quickly had a full list of people to call and coach every month. Then I decided to raise my fee yet again, and soon thereafter I had more clients. Within no time, I hated my life because my phone was always stuck to my ear. I loved coaching but needed more variety and flexibility. So I raised my prices again. At some point, I was actually charging $5,000 an hour.

Why in the world would someone pay *anyone* that much money for one hour? It's simple—it's not about the minutes in the hour but the difference in your life. If someone gives you ideas, information, strategies, and connections that can advance you forward in life and business, you aren't looking at your watch and wallet.

For example, how much money would you spend to have an hour with a person who could radically improve the quality of your life for the rest of your life? How about a meeting with a person who had achieved a million dollars more than you had, in your same business, and was willing to tell you exactly how?

I like to share this metaphor. Imagine you meet a woman on the street who is obviously much happier than you. As she adjusts the briefcase in her hands containing a million in cash, she says, "Hey, I made a million dollars doing what you do, and I did it in one year with half the resources you have. Would you be willing to put a thousand dollars in this box if I agreed to go to lunch with you for an hour or so and tell you exactly how I did it, so you can, too?"

Knowing my audience, I'm guessing you are rolling your eyes and would likely call the police in this situation. But you get the idea. Most people in the world would pay a lot of money to learn how to be happier and more successful. And what about those who wouldn't? Simple: Wish them well and move on. They are not your customers—at least, not yet.

This time-versus-value idea operates in everything we do in this industry. It might take you only a day to create and write a great speech, but as a professional speaker you can be paid $10,000 to $50,000 per speech. If you give just five speeches in a year, was your time well spent?

Most would say yes. You can spend two weeks creating a weekend seminar but charge $1,000 per ticket and get 500 people to attend, making a cool $500,000. You can spend a month planning and shooting videos for an online training program and then register 1,000 people at $100. That's $100,000 in a month. Time has little meaning when you are relating and creating in the expert world.

I know all this sounds out of reach for most people. But you will see in Chapter Six, "The Millionaire Messenger's Money Map," how quickly you can add value and potentially make $1,000,000 just by packaging your how-to advice and doing basic information marketing.

Without a doubt, I will be criticized for offering numbers and talking about money in this way, but again, I think it's important for people to see the possibilities. You and I both know that some people will find success here and others will not. We all have different experience, skills, talents, resources, and so on. I also know, after training tens of thousands of people just like you, that it is possible to become a highly paid expert, and it is surprisingly easy to begin. This book will prove that point just as we have proved it at Experts Academy for years.

7. You don't need a big team.

A dominant myth in our industry is that you need a big team to succeed. Surely, the guesswork goes, you must need a crack team of sales and marketing professionals to reach millions of people . . . right? This is an easy assumption to make, especially when you see your favorite gurus all over television and the Internet.

The reality is a very different picture, though, and something I learned firsthand. I remember attending a conference in 2007 held by Mark Victor Hansen, of *Chicken Soup for the Soul* fame. At that time Mark and cocreator Jack Canfield had a worldwide phenomenon on their hands, selling over 100 million copies of the book series and selling out events left and right. When I attended their event for authors, hoping to create a similarly successful empire, I went out of my way to meet and become friends with their staff members. I will never forget when I met Lisa, a very kind and laid-back staff member, who told me that Mark's entire staff consisted of around five core team members and employees. A $100–million-plus business of just five employees? I couldn't believe it!

In the next 12 months, I befriended nearly every guru in the personal development and informational marketing industry, and I found out that five employees was not, in fact, the norm. Most gurus had far *fewer* employees, if any at all. The average industry leader hired one to three full-time employees at some point, usually soon after he or she had "made it." Most simply outsourced their needs on a project-by-project basis.

Our industry is perfect for outsourcing. Most experts have short-term needs: Build a website, schedule interviews, shoot videos, respond to customers and fans, book travel, write and post articles, and so on. The dream life that Tim Ferriss painted in *The 4-Hour Workweek,* a life of leisure possible only because of virtual assistants and outsourced contractors, turns out to be a very accurate portrayal of what is reality or what is possible for entrepreneurial experts.

At Experts Academy, there is always a lot of discussion about staffing and outsourcing. At one of our recent events, T. Harv Eker, the *New York Times* best-selling author of *The Millionaire Mind,* shared that he had made a horrible decision in hiring too many people. Like many others, he followed the advice of traditional businesspeople and investors who have no idea how our industry works. I felt Harv's pain as he talked about needing to lay off employees after overhiring.

Here is a viewpoint I have consistently held for three years: Do not hire employees when you begin in this industry, *period.* Learn the skills you need to learn to master your own destiny. Here's my most controversial claim: If you ever have more than 10 employees in this industry, then you are doing one or more of the following: (a) not hiring intelligently, (b) not setting up your infrastructure intelligently, (c) not leading and delegating intelligently, (d) not partnering intelligently, or (e) not outsourcing intelligently.

I understand that sounds flippant, and I admit that if I was saying this 10 years ago, I would be foolish.But it's hard to argue with me now that Thomas Friedman has proved that we live in a flat world, and Daniel Pink has shown that we live in a free-agent nation, and Ferriss has shown us all what is possible with virtual assistants and intelligent delegation. Stack on the ease of outsourcing that eLance.com brought us, the advent of the print-on-demand manufacturing and distribution model, and the worldwide move to all things digital, and it's clear that the new business model for experts calls for few real employees—if any. Not only can I logically make this case, but at a tactical level, I have proved it in my own business and in the businesses of many of my clients. Personally, I built a multimillion-dollar expert business without a single employee, and I never hired a full-time team member until I cleared over $2 million in revenue.

Bottom line: Do not fear the staff monster. Because of this fear, thousands of would-be experts stop in their tracks before ever starting. You can become a master in this industry, and you can do it with minimal staffing expenses.

8. The tools for success are simple and cheap.

The low barrier to entry into the expert industry, thanks to outsourcing, has been lowered even more by the advent of simple, cheap, and often free online tools and software programs that allow experts to spread their advice and message around the world.

There was a time when the tools needed to succeed in the expert space were out of reach for most people. These tools included fancy websites, pricey customer-relationship management (CRM) software, expensive public relations companies, hands-off product manufacturers, large retail chains that guarded their gates from our products, and thousand-dollar-plus studio time to record videos and audio programs.

How times have changed! With a few mouse clicks, any expert anywhere in the world can have a website and blog (thanks, WordPress), a social community (thanks, Facebook), a public relations outlet (thanks again, Facebook, and your attention-deficit cousin, Twitter), a television station broadcasting around the world (thanks, YouTube), built-in recording software on all new computers (thanks, Apple), and an online storefront to accept money (thanks, PayPal, Google Checkout, and Yahoo Small Business, to name but a few).

The new reality presented in the preceding paragraph is one of the top reasons I felt it was time to write and release this book: The barrier to entry in the expert space hasn't been lowered—it's been *destroyed*. It isn't just what we can do online now that impresses me; it's also what we can do in terms of creating, manufacturing, and distributing, and fulfilling *products*. Less than a decade ago, experts had to go into very expensive sound or television studios to record their audio- and video-training products. Then they had to have those recordings edited at a cost of thousands of dollars and, finally, sent to a manufacturer that demanded large order quantities to give them a decent deal. Once created, products had to be shipped to distributors who would try to get our programs into stores and would take care of the picking, packing, and shipping of the products.

Today, this process has become cheap, easy, and fast. I can record an audio program from my computer or a video program from a simple-to-use hundred-dollar camera. Then I can e-mail the file to a manufacturer who helps me design the product and also physically creates and ships the resulting how-to product. Here is what's most impressive: Manufacturers and distributors are essentially the same in our industry today, and they do not require us to create a ton of products that sit in a warehouse while we hope for orders to come in. Instead, in what is known as print-on-demand technology, manufacturers don't print any of your products until somebody buys them. No inventory exists until a customer hits the checkout button on your website. And once they do, *bang*, the product is manufactured and shipped the same day, without your lifting a finger. This was the game changer in our industry.

Another innovation was customer-relationship management (CRM) software. The ability to capture customer name and e-mails (leads), follow up with an automated sequence of e-mails (called *autoresponders*), and process customer orders online used to be something only well-established companies could afford. The days of horrifically hard tech setup and custom software integration ended with the bubble burst at the turn of the new century. Today, you can have an online storefront and shopping cart set up in one hour for around $100 a month.

The evolution of blogs and online content management programs has also changed the game and allowed us to easily create incredibly lucrative membership sites. It works like this: You put a bunch of how-to information and training content online for people to access either instantly or at specific times, and people pay you to access the site, thus becoming members. With online membership sites, you don't even have to create physical products anymore, and our industry is moving more and more to the online delivery model. I recently had over 1,000 new customers sign up to access a members-only site that contained how-to information for building an expert empire. It happens all the time in this industry.

9. Financial income is disproportionate to any other industry.

We've already talked about the incredible financial rewards of being an expert, so it isn't necessary to hammer this point further.

But before I show you how to become an expert in the next chapter, and then how you might make your first million dollars in the chapter after that, here are a few points that may help.

First, hard as it may be, you have to readjust your conception of money. To most people, money is a taboo topic. But if you choose this career, you are now in the *business* of sharing your message with the world. And businesspeople talk about money. People will ask you how much you charge, how much you make, how much you keep. You will also have to start sharing details about your life with others if it is relevant to your topic. If you teach anything about making money or having financial abundance, people will naturally want to know about your own results in that area. So get used to it.

You may also need to seriously reexamine your associations and ambitions related to money. What you learned about money from your parents, community, and the media may no longer serve you if you now have grander visions for helping more people in the world and, yes, making more money in return.

Dealing with the concept of money was very difficult for me personally—and, to be honest, sometimes still is. Today I can send out an e-mail and make $100,000 very quickly. I regularly turn away clients who want to pay me $50,000 a year for coaching. I am paid more to speak for one hour at a conference than my parents made in an entire year. I say this not to brag but to point out something weird that you may come to relate to: Helping people and making money at the same time can make us feel *guilty, embarrassed,* and *uneasy.*

I know no one reads that last paragraph and says, "Oh, the poor dear! Brendon feels bad because he has so much money!" So let's turn the lens from me to you for a moment.

What would massive wealth mean to you? Would it be easy to explain to your family and friends? Would they be okay with your being a big-name guru? Would your current money mind-set and conditioning allow you to keep your newfound wealth, or would you lose it as quickly as all those lottery winners do?

It's interesting—and important—to think about this. Guilt, embarrassment, and unease were my first reactions to wealth because of the way I was exposed (perhaps underexposed) to money.

I grew up in a small town, Butte, Montana. A century ago, Butte was a burgeoning metropolis—one of the first five cities in the world to have electricity. You see, Butte was sitting on a massive lode of copper, and before steel took over, copper was king. Butte exploded with immigrants and miners from all around the world, especially Ireland. As happens in all hard-labor industries, an immediate distrust between the workers and "those rich people" quickly emerged. But soon copper would poison the land, steel and aluminum would become more reliable and desirable, and Butte would descend into a long downward economic spiral. To this day, hanging over the town like the specter of death, is a mile-deep, mile-wide pit of toxic waste from mining. Flocks of birds die when they land in it, and there is no way to render the stuff harmless, making the Berkeley Pit above Butte one of the world's biggest environmental disasters. To this day, people with money are looked upon with distrust—a look that says, "Those rich people—made their fortunes on the backs of the poor." I know. I used to look at wealthy people that way.

We lived in Butte when I was very young, and it wasn't until much later in life that I discovered how tough we had it. I do remember one winter when the heater in our house broke. In Butte, it's common for the temperature to drop to 10 to 30 degrees F. below zero, so this was a life-threatening situation. To deal with the problem, my mom and dad grabbed the camping tent out of the garage and set it up in our tiny living room. Then they threw all the sleeping bags and blankets and parkas they could into the tent, and we all huddled in there for something like two weeks. Of course, we kids didn't know it was such a dire situation, even though Mom ended up cooking dinner on Bunsen burners when our electricity went out in the storm. Instead, we kids went strutting into school announcing how cool we were because we were camping in our house! Upon sharing this memory decades later, my mom said to us, "Didn't you know we were camping because the heater was broke, and we were waiting for our next paychecks to come in so we could afford to fix it?"

A silly story, I know, but it illustrates how we grew up. We grew up with nothing, no real material stuff, but we grew up with total abundance because of my parents' resourcefulness. It amazes me to this day how well they managed with four kids.

But in the environment where I grew up, we never talked about money unless it was the stressful kind of talk. The "money blueprint" in my mind essentially said, "We don't need money, because we can get by, and besides, no one likes rich people." That's a very different credo from the one I've had to adopt as a businessperson who says, "Profit wildly so you can continue to reach more people with your message."

In earning greater wealth, I have felt guilty for having more than I need—because of my background and also because I see others out there with just as important a message who are struggling. That is why I have turned my guilt into galvanization to help others find and share their voice. This has helped me overcome any awkwardness about building wealth because it has also tied that act to making a difference in people's lives.

As a final thought, everyone I have ever met has an uneasiness with making (or keeping) money. Volumes could be written about why we need stability and certainty in our financial lives. Instead, let me leave you with a simple thought: If people spent as much time worrying about how to make a difference as they do about how they could make money, then they would soon find themselves rich beyond belief.

I hope this chapter has provided some insight into what being an entrepreneurial expert means: the calling itself and the lifestyle. You can have an extraordinary lifestyle and business simply by sharing your message with others. Do it well enough, and one day you become a Millionaire Messenger.

Chapter Four

YOU: ADVICE GURU

I have been teaching people just like you how to succeed as an expert for quite a while now—long enough to know that you already have questions about how all this works, and about whether you can really be an "expert" on anything. In this chapter, I will share how easy it is to become an expert and add value to people in a way that changes their lives or helps them achieve more in any area.

So let's get to the most pressing question on your mind and the most frequently asked question I get from fans around the world:

"Brendon, how could I possibly be considered an expert, and who would want to listen to me anyway?"

To this question I have a three-part response.

The Results Expert

First, never forget that on the highway of life, you have come further than many others, and the lessons you have learned are both helpful and valuable to others.

At this point in your life, you know how to tie your shoes, but others who are years younger don't. You know how to drive a car; others don't. You might know how to get a job, while others do not. You may know how to get promoted, sew a blanket, get a great deal on a car, write a song, produce a movie, create a blog, get out of debt, lose some weight, improve your marriage, lead others, deal with criticism, give birth to a child, manage employees, ace an exam, find an agent, overcome fear, care for a sick loved one, give a good speech, buy a house, find the perfect clothing style, resume a normal life after a serious illness, or nearly anything you can think of. Others may not.

By the simple act of having accomplished some fundamental tasks in life, you have built what I call "accidental expertise." You might not consider yourself an expert, but the truth is that other people are out there, in the millions, trying to figure out something you probably already know casually. Just as a child looks with amazement at an adult who can tie a shoe—something they have yet to figure out but deeply value—others can look at you *and pay you for* what you already know.

If you sat down and listed all the things you have learned and experienced in life and business, you would find that you know a lot. As a matter of fact, you'd be shocked at how long that list really is. This act would lead you to realize that you are, in fact, what I call a "results expert"—someone who has "been there, done that" and now can teach "that" to others.

What is remarkable here is that millions of people will pay good money to get basic advice and knowledge from you on an enormous range of topics.

I know it can seem a stretch, but think about it: Have you ever paid money to learn how to create a good résumé (I'll bet you bought a book on it), bought an audio program to motivate yourself (I've done this), or used your credit card to pay for access to some training or information online (who hasn't?). While those may have been unremarkable moments for you, they were all examples of the "expert economy" at work. Someone knew how to do something, and you paid them for that knowledge. They had gotten the result you wanted, and so you paid them to take some months or years off your learning curve. You paid for information that could help you get from point A on life's highway to point B. You paid for results. It's as simple as that.

So the question is, what results have you gotten in life and business?

At this point, a lot of people who hire me as a coach often say, "But, Brendon, I don't know what results I've gotten, and I don't know what expertise I have."

To these people I gently reply, "Yes, the fact is, you do know. All the answers lie within you." Then, to prove this to them, I often give them a sentence-completion activity. I write the start of a sentence and let them finish it. For example, I will give them a statement that says, "The secrets I have learned to having a happy marriage are…" It's amazing how fast they can complete the sentence. They'll immediately say, "Listen more," or

"Show more appreciation," or "Give respect," or "Schedule date nights." Most clients are surprised at how immediately they know exactly how to finish the sentence. They feel a renewed sense of confidence and competence as they discover that they have all the answers within them.

I'm going to give you similar sentence-completion activities throughout this book, which I call *Expert Signposts*. When you complete these simple yet profound statements, you will start to discover topics and ideas that can be the base of your new expert empire.

Below are a few statements that I want you to complete right now. So stop, grab your journal, write down each statement, and finish it as honestly and thoroughly as you can.

Expert Signposts:

1. Five things I have learned about motivating myself and achieving my dreams are...

2. Five things I have learned about leading others and being a good team player are...

3. Five things I have learned about managing money are...

4. Five things I have learned about having a successful business are...

5. Five things I have learned about marketing a product or brand are...

6. Five things I have learned about being a good partner in an intimate relationship are...

7. Five things I have learned about spirituality or connecting with a higher power are...

8. Five things I have learned about home decorating/fashion/organizing are...

9.   Five things I have learned about managing my life and being effective are…

I know this activity might have seemed silly, and that not all these statements were relevant or easy for you to complete, but guess what I just helped you do? I helped you brainstorm what you could teach others in the nine most lucrative topics in the expert industry:

- Motivation Advice
- Leadership Advice
- Financial Advice
- Business Advice
- Marketing Advice
- Relationship Advice
- Spiritual Advice
- Style Advice
- Productivity Advice

Now, please don't worry if this seemed difficult or irrelevant to you. I'm just seeding a few ideas in your mind now, and in the coming chapters I will help you gain greater clarity and insight.

For now, the point is to begin realizing that you have figured some things out in life because you have learned some hard lessons and because you have gotten some results. Does that make sense to you?

Finally, don't worry if you want to be an expert in an area you have *yet to get results in.* Of course, you will eventually want to get as many results as you can, but it isn't always a requirement. I'll explain this concept next.

The Research Expert

Here is the next part in my three-part response to "Brendon, how could I possibly be considered an expert, and who would want to listen to me anyway?"

Second, never forget that experts are students first and that you can go research any topic and become an "expert" in that area, starting now.

I learned the value of this point by accident.

While I was in college, my little sister Helen, whom I adore with all my heart, was having relationship trouble. She had been engaged, and her relationship with her fiancé started falling apart. Because she and I are so close, she came to me for advice. This would seem silly given that I was single and had never had a successful relationship myself, at least not at the level of being engaged or married. There's a hidden message here: People ask those they trust for advice. I certainly was not a "relationship expert," but I desperately wanted to help my little sister. So what did I do?

I did what I always do when someone asks me for help on any given topic: I became a researcher. I can vividly recall the day Helen asked me for help and how horribly bumbling I was in giving her any decent advice. That night, frustrated with my ignorance, I drove to the bookstore and spent four hours reading everything I could on relationships. I left the store with a legal pad full of notes and over a dozen books on the topic. I spent the next week reading and synthesizing everything I learned. The next time my sister asked for advice, boy did she get an earful!

Then something interesting happened. Like buying a red car and then suddenly seeing red cars everywhere, I started hearing everyone talk about their relationship problems. I would share what I knew with them, and suddenly I became an "expert" on relationships on my campus. One day I helped a student who happened to be in a sorority with her relationship issues, and a week later she asked me to come speak to her entire sorority on the topic. *And they paid me $300 for that speech!* I was so nervous about that speech that I nearly lost my lunch on the way to the sorority house.

Those two experiences taught me about another type of expert: the "research expert."

Did you know that you don't need to have ever *done* something to be considered an expert in it? You don't have to be a "results expert." This seems an outlandish claim, but have you ever seen an academic on television being interviewed about business? They aren't even *in* business, and they may never have *practiced* business principles, but because they studied business closely enough and knew about *best practices* in business, they were considered experts.

Just as I became an expert on relationships without ever having been married, you can be seen as an expert on any given topic without necessarily having achieved any results in that area. Because this sounds like blasphemy to so many, I have created a rock-solid set of questions that changes people's perspective very quickly. Here they are:

1. If you were about to invest in real estate, would you take advice from someone who had never owned a home or commercial property?

Most people reply, "Absolutely not."

But then I ask,

2. But what if that person who had never owned a property had interviewed in detail the top 20 billionaire real estate investors in the world and distilled all their lessons into a 10-step system? Would you listen then?

Of course, everyone changes their mind and gets the point. If someone has researched a given topic and broken it down for us, we will listen. And we will pay for their guidance.

Let me give you a famous example from our "expert industry."

Have you read Napoleon Hill's famous book *Think and Grow Rich*? If you haven't, you must. The book is about how to build a wealthy life and has been called one of the most influential wealth and achievement books in history. Generations have called it one of the most pivotal books of their lives, and it has sold millions of copies worldwide.

What is fascinating about this example is that by all accounts, Napoleon Hill was never financially rich and never a wild success himself, by many measures (certainly not before writing the book). So how could he have become one of the most influential experts and authors in the history of our industry? The answer is simple: He researched and reported on his topic.

The story behind *Think and Grow Rich* is that Napoleon Hill *interviewed* rich people like Andrew Carnegie and Carnegie's wealthy friends. From these interviews, Hill simply *synthesized* what they were saying, finding the common threads of their conversations, and *distilled* the lessons they learned and *best practices* into *useful chunks of information* that helped "regular" people understand the topic. People paid and continue to pay for this book because it can improve their lives and take years off their learning curve.

That is the process of being a research expert: Choose a topic that people find valuable, research it, interview others on it, synthesize what you learn, and then offer your findings for sale so others can learn and improve their lives.

When you understand this point, a whole world of topics opens up for you. With enough research, you can become an expert on any topic in the world. I find that idea freeing, because you can actually *choose* what topic you want to help others with, and then go out and master it.

I often get harpooned for saying this, so let me make a few caveats and clarifications. I'm not suggesting that you go out there and claim to be an expert on something you don't know. I'm not saying to hang out your shingle as an expert on a topic you casually researched on Google one day. Everything I suggest to you in this book is offered under the assumption that you are a good person, that you act with integrity, that you really want to help people, that you are a dedicated to excellence, and that you would never claim to be something you are not. I believe in hard work, in mastering your topic, and in serving others with integrity and transparency. I have built my career on those principles, and you will, too, if you truly want to succeed.

Now back to the story and back to our *Expert Signposts*. Stop now and complete the following starter sentences:

1. A topic I have always been passionate about is…

2. A topic I would like to help other people master is…

3. If I could research any topic in the world and help people master it, that topic would be…

4. The reason I think people need help in this area is…

5. To start researching this topic more, I could…

6. People I could interview on this topic include…

Again, these are simply starter statements to get you thinking. There are no right or wrong answers. The point of my sharing these activities is to seed your mind for later concepts and strategies that I will share with you. So don't get overwhelmed or worry about what you're going to claim as your area of expertise just yet.

The Role Model

So far I have covered these two points:

First, never forget that you have come further than some others on the highway of life, and the lessons you have learned are helpful and valuable to others.

Second, never forget that experts are students first and that you can go research any topic and become an expert in that area, starting now.

The first point illustrates that we all follow experts who have "been there, done that." The second reminds us that we also follow those who are deeply knowledgeable about an area because they have researched it more than we have.

Here's one more insight:

Third, never forget that people listen to those they trust, respect, admire, and follow—they listen to role models.

This is obvious but cannot be overstressed. If people believe you are a good person, they will ask you for all sorts of advice.

Think about it: Have you ever listened to someone's advice even though you knew they were not an "expert"? Of course you have. You cut your arm and listened to your mom, who was no doctor, about how to "fix it." Your friend told you that your car engine sounded funny, so you took it to the shop. Your poor friend told you about a wealth opportunity, and you gave it a try. Your overweight neighbor said to eat more vegetables and you thought, "I'll give it a shot."

I am always amazed at how this concept shows up in my life. Millions of people have seen me online, on television, in print, and in person. For whatever reason, many of them reach out to me in areas that I have no clue about, often offering to pay me tens of thousands of dollars for my "expertise."

For example, I have been offered $500,000 to help a man I never met restructure his company, and I'm not an expert on structuring companies. A woman offered me $2,000 a month to coach her through her divorce, despite the fact that I know nothing about divorce, divorce law, or the emotional realities of going through that process. I have been paid $15,000 to give a leadership speech, with the only condition being that I had to add a few lines about diversity to fit a conference theme, even though diversity is not my expertise and I am a gangly white kid from Montana—not exactly a cultural Mecca or a melting pot of diversity.

While these are extraordinary, even bizarre, examples, this type of thing happens all the time to people in the public eye who have earned a good reputation. Business owners, speakers, authors, celebrities, bloggers, YouTubers, and leaders in every field and in every industry are constantly asked for their advice and offered money for expertise, consulting, coaching, or content that is completely beyond their realm of knowledge, skill, experience, or ability.

Why? Because people ask advice from people they trust, respect, admire, and follow. Put simply, people seek out good people for information.

On a personal level, I'd pay a boatload of money to get business advice from the Dalai Lama, even though that isn't his field of expertise. I'd listen to every word Tony Robbins tells me on *any* topic, even if he's stretching for it. If Barack Obama told me I should move to China, I'd at least have to think about it. I, like everyone else, listen to people I admire.

Why am I bringing this up here? I do it to drive home the fact that if you are seen as a role model, you will find that your status is an incredibly powerful pillar in positioning yourself as an expert. This is my way of saying to you, *Be a good person and good things will follow.*

Frankly, I think we need more role models in society in general. We need more people living lives of integrity, compassion, and service, and I believe the future belongs to those who live such lives. Business and abundance flow to those who know how to live a good life and serve others.

Expert Signposts:

1. One reason people might admire me is because…

2. I have tried to live a good life by living by the following principles...

3. When people look at my life, they can point to the fact that I have done good things, such as...

4. The traits that make me a good person and that I will show to the world include...

The "Guru Trifecta"

I had a hidden agenda in introducing you to these three pillars of expertise: results expert, research expert, and role model.

Now that you know them, I want you to build these pillars consciously, strategically, and actively for the rest of your life on any topic in which you want to help others. When all these pillars are strong and aligned, you will have reached a level of expertise and trust that makes you incredibly respected and in demand.

In my business, I am always trying to research my topics more deeply, seeking to achieve more results in the areas I am teaching, and striving to be a good role model for those I serve. I work very hard at it, and it is always on my mind. I believe that doing these things has been the secret to my success. A lot of "experts" and "gurus" out there stop learning and applying, and because they do that, they stop being able to offer the best advice to others, and they start to see their businesses fail.

I'm always asking up-and-coming experts these questions: Have *you* diligently researched the topic you want to help others learn or master? Have you read at least six books on the topic in the past year? Have you interviewed at least ten other experts on the topic? Have you applied your lessons learned and gotten significant results? Are you living a good life that people will admire and respond to?

When you combine researcher, results maker, and role model, you have a magic that transcends the word "expert" and elevates you to *trusted adviser*. People start thinking of you as a "guru" on your topic (in the positive sense of the word, making you "one who spreads light and wisdom"). Suddenly people start asking you for advice all the time, and thus, you can have a real business serving others with your advice, knowledge, and expertise.

How can you have a real business doing this? How do researchers, results makers, and role models actually get paid for their information? We'll cover that in the next chapter.

Chapter Five

10 STEPS TO AN EXPERT EMPIRE

Now that you know you can gain "expert" status by getting results in that area, researching your topic, and being a good role model, let's get tactical. How do you get your message out there, and what do experts and gurus actually do to build their empires? It is shockingly simple.

It turns out that almost every entrepreneurial expert and Millionaire Messenger, those who have truly reached millions of people and made millions of dollars, follows the same game plan. This chapter lays out that plan in 10 steps and will serve as your to-do list and launching pad.

Step 1: Claim and Master Your Topic

As straightforward as this first step sounds, I certainly wish I had a dollar every time someone said to me, "Brendon, what topic should I be an expert in?"

This question is quite revealing about our community and the people in it. As an industry, it shows that people generally (and accurately) believe they can learn and gain expertise quickly. *Tell me what to be an expert in,* they seem to say, *and I will go make it happen.* This mentality is especially prevalent in the United States, where higher education has taught and empowered us essentially to choose our careers.

As for the people asking the question, it shows that they are true *creatives,* meaning that they dabble in multiple topics and passions. Most experts I know are actually experts in multiple topics, because their minds and their hearts are intrigued by so many things in this world. Curiosity does not kill the creative; it makes them feel alive. You, too, probably have multiple areas in which you could become an expert. Personally, I have become an expert in not only excelling in the expert industry but also in leadership, motivation, high performance, conflict resolution, mediation, promotional partnerships, corporate sponsorships, nonprofit fund-raising, professional speaking, organizational development, and online marketing. I have million-dollar-plus brands in many of these spaces. While to some this seems out of reach or exhausting, to the creative it is the way of the world—our curiosity, love for learning and continuing education, and desire to master our world has helped us gain great expertise in multiple topics.

But you will discover later in this book that trying to be an everything-under-the-sun expert right from the start is and always will be a *bad strategy*. If you are going to build a real empire, you need to pick one topic, learn it, master it, share it, become known for it, and make real money teaching it. *Then* you have a real foundation on which to build, and *only then* should you start positioning yourself as an expert on other topics. Yes, you heard me—choose *one* topic to be known for, develop a real business on that one topic, and broaden the topic later on. I can share from personal experience and working with thousands of students and dozens of the most committed and financially successful experts in the world that this is the right strategy for beginners: one topic for now.

So what topic are you going to hang your hat on as an expert? As you will recall, you are or can quickly become an expert on any given topic by getting results, doing your research, and serving as a role model. So what will it be? What is your topic?

I know these are painful questions, because they bring to bear the one word that all real creatives hate to hear: *focus*! If you are having a difficult time choosing your topic, let me assist you. If you already know your topic, this will serve as an important decision filter for you.

Choosing a topic to teach others about is akin to choosing a passion in life—sometimes it chooses you more than you choose it. That is why I want to give you a few categories to consider in developing and deciding on your topic.

First, choose to teach others a topic that you *already* find fascinating and *already* love to learn about. If you find yourself always buying and reading leadership books, then there is a hint: leadership may be your topic. If you are always asking mothers what they've learned about good parenting, there's another hint. If you have scores of audio books on sales and marketing on your bookshelves, you already love sales and marketing, so why not decide to go help others learn what you have learned?

Second, choose a topic based on something you *already love to do*. If you look at your past five years and notice that you just love to buy and sell foreclosed houses, then you are already "doing" your topic. What is it that you love to do? What are your passions right now? Those are great starting points for the process of choosing a topic. Perhaps, like Lorie Marrero, you love to organize your and your friends' homes—so you can become a home-organizing expert. Or like Roger Love, you might love to sing and help others sing, so you can become a voice coach.

Third, think about what you have *always wanted to learn*. In every field, every expert began as a student. The best medical doctors in the world, for example, were not expert doctors to begin with. They were students first, then practitioners, and then experts. The nice part about the advice and how-to industry is that you can become an expert on any given topic, which means you can choose to reinvent yourself anytime you like. You define the terms of your career, and you choose the work and the topic of your work. I find that incredibly empowering. So what would you love to learn about and then go out and teach others once you have gotten results, researched it, or become a role model?

Fourth, consider what you have *been through in life*. Have you had a turning point, a triumph, or a tragedy that makes you say, "Wow, I struggled through something important, and now I want to teach others so that I can minimize their struggles." Have you had life or work experiences that gave you a unique story, skill set, or perspective that you would like to share? Sometimes the easiest way to discover signposts for what we should do now or in the future is to look under the milestones of our past. I decided to make my car accident and the resulting life transformation the foundational inspiration for my work and for my interest and expertise in human potential.

Finally, choose a topic that you are willing to speak about and *live and breathe* for at least the next five years. I cannot stress the importance of this enough. A woman once stood up at one of my seminars, crying, and said she hated the hole she'd dug for herself in her expert career. She shared that some "marketing guru" had told her that since a family member of hers had committed suicide, it was her calling to help others learn about and prevent suicide. So this poor woman traveled the country speaking about suicide to youth audiences for years, all the while having to retell and relive the story of her little sister's suicide. By the end of a few years, she was a recognized expert but now hated the topic she had chosen, even though it made a difference in people's lives. The moral of the story is to choose your topic wisely. You'll be researching your topic, reading books, interviewing other experts, writing articles and blog posts, shooting videos, and sharing your message *for years*. So decide on a topic you absolutely love.

Expert Signposts:

1. The topics I have always studied and been fascinated with in my life are…

2. The things I love to do in my life are…

3. Something I have always wanted to go out and learn more about is…

4. Things I have been through in my life that might inspire people or instruct them on how to live a good life or grow a good business include the time I went through…

5. Based on these ideas, the topics I would love to gain expertise in and make a career helping others with include…

6. The topic I would want to start with first and build a real career and business around is…

Step 2: Pick Your Audience

Many marketers in our community will read my first step and say I have gotten it all wrong. They will say, "Pick your niche audience first, not your topic. Find a buying base of customers and find out what *they want*—not what *you want* to give or teach them—and then serve them with what they want." I agree with this to a degree. But I have learned that this is often a chicken-or-the-egg dilemma for most up-and-coming experts. There is not a "right" way, so whether you start with step 1 (pick your topic) or step 2 (pick your audience) is not terribly relevant.

What *is* relevant here is that you ultimately decide *whom you want to serve most* in your new career. Do you want to help youth, parents, women, men, retirees, businesses, nonprofits, entrepreneurs—who, exactly, is your target audience? Once you have a demographic in mind, go another level deeper and consider your ideal audience's age, including what they have been through in life, what personality types they embody, and what they do for a living. The best practice is to narrow your audience to a recognizable type of person.

With that said, let me speak to the likely question, "Brendon, I just have an important message, man, and it can help everyone in the world. Do I really have to define and box in my audience?" To this I often reply, "Yes, you do. It is admirable that your message can help so many people, and I believe it can help most people, but the challenge is that you do not have the *time* and the *resources* to market to the entire world, even if the entire world needs your stuff. You have to target an audience, not only because it is likely that only a narrow audience of people really *needs and will buy* your message but also because *you* need to create effective and realistic promotions. You can't advertise or market to the entire world, so pick a group and type of person to start with.

Choosing an audience is akin to choosing your topic in that you want to find people similar to you. Who is passionate about the same topics you are? Who wants to learn the same things you do? Who has been through similar life struggles to yours? Here are more questions to consider.

Expert Signposts:

1. The audience that would most likely benefit from training on a topic like mine is…

2. The audience that would most likely pay for training on a topic like mine is…

3. The audience of people who seem underserved on my topic includes…

4. People who need education on my topic often belong to organizations like...

Step 3: Discover Your Audience's Problems

All experts are students and servants first, so it is necessary for you to study your audience, discover their needs, and serve them with advice and how-to information that can solve their problems and improve their lives.

At Experts Academy, I share dozens of ways to get to know your audience's needs and buying behaviors, but I want to share with you here what I call my "Customer Insight Formula." The formula consists of four simple questions I like to begin with when meeting or surveying my ideal audience so that I can better understand and serve them. Here are questions you can ask your audience in order to learn more about what they need from you:

1. What is it you are trying to accomplish this year?
2. What do you think it would take to double your business (or happiness) this year?
3. What frustrates you the most about your business or your life right now?
4. What have you already tried to do to improve your situation? What worked and what didn't work?

Answers to these questions help me understand the ambitions, needs, frustrations, and learning preferences of my clients.

In general, the more you understand your audience and their most pressing problems and ambitions, the more you are able to create targeted problem-solving how-to information that they will buy and consume. The better you know what your audience needs, the more you can give them information that improves their lives.

Below are more questions to help you think through your audience's lives and how you might serve them.

Expert Signposts:

1. My audience often dreams of achieving...

2. My audience is afraid of not knowing enough about...

3. My audience often searches and Googles phrases like...

4. My audience likes to follow these types of people and organizations in the media or through social media...

5. My audience hates having to do things like...

6. My audience often pays good money for...

7. If I could give my audience any information that would help them improve their lives, they would probably want strategies on how to...

8. The steps my audience often misses when trying to achieve their goals include...

9. Based on all these ideas, some how-to information that I could provide to my audience that would make them very happy would include strategies on how to...

Step 4: Define Your Story

I ask all my clients a very straightforward but powerful question, "What is a story of struggle from your past that could illustrate to your audience that you have struggled through something similar to what they are struggling through?" That story, even more than fancy degrees or a lifetime of success in your topic or industry, is often the central piece in conveying credibility.

Oddly, we tend to relate to one another's struggles more than to our successes. Thus, we have to look for rapport points defined by a shared experience of challenges so that we can connect with our audiences. In other words, your audience wants to know that you've been through what they've been through.

This point often confounds up-and-coming experts from Western cultures. For example, in the United States, our culture has taught us to boast about all our accomplishments in order to gain credibility. We are supposed to list our degrees, certifications, achievements, memberships, and any accomplishment or affiliations that can make us "look good." Because of this, many new experts will often start their promotions or biographies by bragging about how wonderfully talented and powerful they are. But let me ask you a question: Have you ever been on a date with someone who just bragged about how great they were? Did you relate to them? Did you want to engage them in dialogue? Probably not.

People often relate initially to those in the expert industry based on our story of struggle. After that—after they believe in who we are and what we have been through—they're interested in what we know and what we have accomplished.

You see, every audience that hears about you and hears about your expert career wonders, "Who *is* this person? What have they been through, overcome, figured out, succeeded at? Based on all that, what can they teach me that will help me improve my life?"

Notice the ordering of that question, as I have found it to be very purposeful and powerful. Audiences want to know, in this order:

1. Who are you and what have you been through in life that I can relate to in my own life?
2. What have you overcome and how?
3. What did you figure out along the way?
4. What did you succeed at—what results did you get?
5. What are you going to teach me that I can apply now to make my life better?

Because these are the questions that every audience asks when hearing from any expert, you need to work out your responses to them. Then you need to address these questions in every communication you ever send to new prospects or audience members. The length of your responses is not as important as the need for your heart and sincerity to shine through everything you say and do.

Expert Signposts:

1. A story of struggle from my past that my audience might relate to is...

2. Something I have overcome in my life that others might find inspiring or feel a connection with is...

3. The main lessons I have learned from my journey include...

4. Accomplishments and affiliations I have in my life that help further my credibility include...

5. Lessons I can teach people that will help them in my topic area and their life situation include...

Step 5: Create a Solution

Now that you have begun thinking through your topic, audience, and personal credibility story, it's time to create a product or program—a solution—that your audience can follow (and buy) to get where they want to go.

This is where most people fail in our industry. Everyone wants to make a difference and make an income as an advice guru and expert, but few will ever *do the work* of sitting down and creating the how-to program or system to sell to their audience. They never write the book, craft the speech, create the seminar, set up a coaching program, or shoot the videos for their online training course.

In part, many people never create their how-to programs because they simply don't know where to begin, or they get overwhelmed by the bad advice in our industry (and there's a lot of it).

I will make it easy for you, though. To begin, you simply have to choose *how* you would like your customer to receive your information. There are only five main ways, or modalities, by which people can learn from you. Knowing these modalities will help you think though how you would like to deliver your information to your audience.

The first way that people can consume your information is through *reading it*. This means you can create written how-to solutions like books, eBooks, workbooks, articles, newsletters, blog postings, instructor guides, and transcripts.

Second, your audience might want to *hear* your information, which can lead you to creating audio CDs, MP3s, conference call series, or one-on-one calls.

Third, people may want to watch your information on their television, computer, or mobile device. That means you might create DVD home-study programs, online videos and webinars, and mobile video apps.

Fourth, your fans and consumers might want to *experience* you and your information in person, which would lead you to create live events like seminars, workshops, retreats, adventures, and expos.

Finally, a segment of your audience will always want to *master* your information and get a greater degree of access and training from you. To serve them, you might create exclusive mastermind programs, coaching services, and mentorship programs.

So those are the ways people might consume your information—they will want to read it, hear it, watch it, experience it, or master it over a longer term. Many will want all these things, so it is your job to decide which modality you would like to teach in and which modality or modalities you would like to bundle to create your solution. In general, it is also helpful to know that the further we move in this modality continuum, from reading it to mastering it, the more value people associate with the modality, and the more you can charge. For example, people see a live three-day seminar as more valuable than a book, and they are thus willing to pay more for it.

The bottom line, though, is that in order to serve your clients and make money in this industry, you *must* create a program for sale. Thousands of people will want to buy your brains and your advice. Since there's only one of you, creating a solution that they can access and buy is critical to your success and to perpetuating your message.

So what kind of solution would you like to create first for your audience? A book? An audio program? A video-based training program? A live training event? A coaching program? There is no right or wrong answer, but it is absolutely critical that you choose one and create something to sell to people if you are going to serve them.

If any of this seems overwhelming to you, don't worry. In the next chapter, I will show you a simple million-dollar plan that mixes these modalities effectively and does not require you to sell tens of thousands of products in order to earn a substantial income.

The next step in creating your solution, of course, is creating the *content* to go into your products and programs. This is one of our most popular topics at Experts Academy—the *how* of creating great how-to information and training. The basics of my approach are to figure out what your audience needs to know in order to move from point A to point B in their lives. What process or step-by-step approach would they have to take to achieve their goals? Start thinking through that and you will discover a lot of your actual content and how to organize it. From there, you drill down into each step and share examples, common obstacles, success secrets, and so on. You essentially create a how-to solution that they can follow to success. That is the expert content creation process at a high level.

Expert Signposts:

1. When my audience learns my information, they will probably want to learn it through these modalities the most…[choices: reading, hearing, watching, experiencing, mastering]

2. The modality I would like to teach in the most involves my… [choices: writing it, speaking it for audio, presenting it on video, training at a live event, or coaching over a period of time]

3. Based on these ideas, I think the first how-to product or program I will create for my audience will be something like…

4. To achieve results, my customers will need how-to information that helps them move from point A, just beginning, to point B, arriving at their destination. The steps they would have to take on that journey are…

5. As my customers take these steps, they will have to keep in
   mind...

6. Common mistakes people make as they take these steps iclude...

7. An outline for my new how-to solution for my customers could
   look like this...[Yes, create your outline for your new product or
   program now!]

Step 6: Put up a Website

Now that you have a message, audience, story, and solution, it's time
to get online and start cultivating a following and building a business that
promotes your advice and how-to program.

Thanks to modern technology, for anyone with a computer, creating
a decent website is no longer a barrier to entry. My job here is not to tell
you that you need a website—you already know that. It is also not to tell
you *how* to build a website. There are many free website building tools out
there, as well as superlow-cost Web designers via Elance.com.

Instead, let me share three things your website *must do* to begin building
your expert empire.

First, your website must add value. This should be a no-brainer in today's
society, but it isn't. The point of having an expert website is to provide
valuable information to those who need it. But if people visit your website
and see nothing there but random musings about life, your Twitter posts
about walking the dog, or a full rundown of your services and prices, then
you aren't adding value and you will get nowhere fast.

What consumers expect from an expert and a website has changed
significantly in the past five years. Today your site visitors want to see blog
posts, articles, and videos that add value to their lives. They don't want
to see you brag about who you are, talk about how much you charge, or
explain what you are doing with your life. They want content and training,
and it is your job to give it to them, for free, on your website in order to
build rapport with them and provide value to them. This is the first rule of
all business: Add value.

Second, your website must capture leads. If your website is adding value to people, then the word will begin to spread, and soon you will have traffic to your website. At that point, one thing must happen: You must capture the names and e-mail addresses of your visitors. You do this by offering free training or resources in exchange for their name and e-mail address. You have seen this at work before: *Sign up for our newsletter and you will instantly receive...*

Capturing leads is a critical best practice because the size of your newsletter list in our industry is almost always directly proportionate to your income and influence. Obviously, once you have a customer's contact information, you can continue to send them free value, deepen your relationship, and, yes, offer them your products and programs for purchase. The more fans, followers, and subscribers you have, the more money you make, leading to our next point.

Third, your website must make money! Another no-brainer, but I am personally shocked at how few experts have a website that effectively features and sells their how-to programs. On your homepage, you should feature your latest products for sale, and when a consumer clicks on the link to learn more, you should have an effective marketing strategy that leads them to buy the product. Basic, right? But how well is your website doing right now in terms of making real money and having an impact on your sales?

Most people say their website is terrible at doing these three things. That is why I created the "Homepage ATM" wireframe for experts to show their Web designers. In one of the free videos that you will receive when you opt in at ExpertsAcademy.com, you and your Web designer will learn how to create an effective website that makes you money while you sleep. The basic idea is to follow the strategies in the next step.

Expert Signposts:

1. If I were to design my ideal website, the value and information I would want to provide to my visitors would be things like...

2. The main thing people would like to learn upon visiting my site is...

3. The free gift I could offer my customers in exchange for their contact information is…

4. The products and programs I want my clients to know about and buy will be…

Step 7: Campaign Your Products and Programs

Once your website is up and the world can now get value from you and buy your products, it's time to draw people in with free value and then, ultimately, to offer something for sale.

I like to use the word "campaign" in this step rather than "promote," because a value-added campaign is fundamentally different from the latter. A promotion is a singular marketing piece or a series of touch points with a customer. It is a promotional postcard or brochure or e-mail that essentially says, "Hey, buy my stuff!" If that doesn't work, it is sent again and again until a customer goes insane.

A value-added campaign, however, is different and the absolute best practice in our industry. To define terms, *a campaign is a strategic sequence of promotions that leads to a desired consumer behavior.* In a typical value-adding campaign in the expert industry, we send out a strategic series of communications to customers that actually serves them with great content. We give these free content pieces, and in the last communication in the series, we effectively say, "*Hey, if you like the free training I have just sent you, then you will love my new program called* [insert your product name here]."

This method of marketing is time-tested in our industry. By delivering real value to customers in advance of asking for a sale, we create the kind of trust, value, and reciprocity that helps consumers feel comfortable in ultimately buying our products and programs.

As an example, in my last major online marketing effort, which generated over $2,000,000 in just 10 days, I sent out three valuable training videos, and then in the fourth video I said, "If you liked that, here are details on my new program that will help you…" Visit my website, subscribe to my list, and you will see how I do all this. It is simpler than most people expect.

Although all this might sound very technical, and it is often overwhelming to newcomers to the industry, take heart; marketing is really that easy these days. Send out good information that improves people's lives, and then say, "Hey, if you liked that, then you will *love* this." That's it in a nutshell. The *critical success factor* is to make sure your *free* information is truly *valuable and actionable*. I don't need to tell you that if your free content is crummy, customers will not want to buy your priced products.

Of course, as part of your campaign, you have to effectively communicate *why* your customers should believe in you and buy from you. You have to cover all the marketing basics of creating rapport, effectively describing your customer's pain points and how your solution overcomes them, sharing your credibility, telling your customer the benefits of your solution, showing testimonials of people who have succeeded by following your advice, and giving a good price and a guarantee. I found that most people are terrible at doing these things, and that is why I structured my seminar the way I did. No program in the world goes into more detail about marketing how-to information than Experts Academy. I can't give you a full course on marketing basics in the limited text of this book. But to help you begin, I have focused this step's *Expert Signposts* on how you can think through developing a campaign and how you can explain the value of your information and programs.

One more point on campaigning: *You never stop campaigning*. As a messenger on a mission, you know that your goal is to get your message out there as far and as wide as possible. If that is true, you should set up campaigns that automatically and always run from your website(s). You should be doing everything you can on a strategic, diligent, and consistent basis to get your message out there.

Expert Signposts:

1. To add value to people before I sell to them, I can send them a few free content pieces like…

2. The first product I want to market to my customers is…

3. The reason people should buy this product is because it helps them…

4. This product ultimately gives customers the following benefits in their life…

5. The reason this product is different from others out there is…

6. The reasons I know this product gets results for people is that it…

7. The reason the price point of this product is fantastic is…

8. To pay the price point of this product, people must believe that…

9. The reason people need to buy this program now is…

Step 8: Post FREE Content

In our new hyperconnected world, two things bring traffic and attention to your work: search and social media. And the one and only thing that is guaranteed to generate the interest of both the search engines and the masses is *content* posted online.

You should be putting online free, high-quality blog postings, articles, podcasts, and, most importantly training videos. By loading these postings with keyword phrases related to your brand, topic, and market, the search engines will start to notice them and rank your sites and content higher on their result pages. As an example, if you post fifteen videos on your topic on YouTube, and you drive traffic to the YouTube pages the videos are posted on, then you'll see those videos start to move up on Google results pages.

Here's a real-world example. Before this book was released, if you typed "Millionaire Messenger" into Google and hit search, no results were generated that had anything to do with the book. Because I didn't have any content out there tagged with "millionaire messenger," Google wasn't able to find any results. So, I shot a twelve-minute video about my book, teaching concepts from this chapter, and posted it on YouTube. Then I posted the link to the Youtube video on my Twitter and Facebook pages, and I also e-mailed the link to my subscribers. Just twenty-four hours later, when anyone Googled the phrase "Millionaire Messenger," my video was right on top of the results.

If you're like most up-and-coming experts, this idea of posting free content online is a little scary. Almost everyone I know is frightened that they're "giving too much advanced stuff away" or that they'll "run out of stuff to teach." Both these concerns simply display a lack of perspective and a misunderstanding about how commerce and creativity really work.

In general, you should give your best advice and ideas away for *free*. Yes, for free. I'm not saying to give *all* your content away for free, but rather to give your best ideas away for free. I often tell people to "lead with your best work" because you often don't get another chance to prove your value. People seem to understand this in other industries, but not our own. For example, few highly paid professionals in the corporate market would get a project assigned to them and say, "Well, I'll just give my average effort to this project, and then next year I'll give them the best I've got." If they did that, they'd find themselves unemployed fairly quickly.

In your efforts, you should be putting out your best and highest-quality content as a "front-end attractor." Simply put, if the stuff people get from you is free and incredible, then they'll be more likely and willing to buy your other products. They think, "Gosh, if this is the caliber of stuff this person gives away for free, then the stuff they're *selling* must be exceptional!"

To address concerns you may have about "running out" of content to teach, take heart. As an expert, you're always learning more about your topic and you're always getting feedback from your customers. Your ideas, perspective, and wisdom will grow with time.

To get started, you should consider posting short articles on your blog (use Wordpress), and content videos on YouTube and Facebook. That will help you get your message out there and start attracting attention. Your content can be any advice or how-to strategies you have on your topic. A friend of mine, Mike Koenigs, often tells his clients to post ten videos on YouTube, each one addressing one question from the ten most frequently asked questions they receive from customers.

The takeaway is that the more great content you post online, whether articles or videos, the more the search engines find you. And you also give your followers great information that they can now help you share through their own social media channels. More content out there, more traffic, more money and exposure for you.

Expert Signposts:

1. Ten short articles I could write and post on my blog include topics such as…

2. Ten short videos I could create and post to YouTube could cover topics such as…

3. The "biggest idea" I have for my customers that I should now share for free via video or articles online is…

4. The keywords I want to emphasize in my article and video posts so that they are optimized to get good search engine results include key phrases such as…

5. When I put all this free content online, my goal is for the customer to read, hear, or watch it and then take this next action…

Step 9: Get Promotional Partners

You can get your message out there only so far by yourself. That's why it is important to start looking for other experts in the community who have audiences that may be interested in your topics and trainings. If you can get those experts to promote your message to their base of fans, followers, and subscribers, then you immediately amplify your message as well as your income.

I am always surprised at how few people do this purposefully and strategically. I have met thousands of people with important messages, stories, and how-to information who never once considered the idea of getting a peer or leader in their industry to promote them. I guess everyone is still just hoping Oprah taps them with her magic wand someday.

For me, I am always attending conferences, networking, researching, and seeking new partners who can help me reach more people with my message. I constantly cold-call and colde-mail "gurus" in various industries and offer to interview them for my audience, help them with their online marketing, or ask how I can be of service. I live by this credo: Give and you shall receive. I believe that if I add value for other people in my industry, then they will reciprocate somehow and someday.

Nothing serves your message more than getting others to promote your message farther and wider than you ever could on your own. So start looking for promotional partners. For the most part, if you are willing to add value and promote the messages of others, many will be willing to do the same for you.

Doing this begins with basic online research. Who are the other experts in your topic area? One quick way to discover this is to Google specific keywords related to your topic. Another clever way is to go to a speakers' bureau website. Just Google "speaker bureau" and see who else is speaking on your topic. The best way to learn of and meet others is to attend conferences in the expert industry—writing conferences, speaker seminars, and so on. Once you have an understanding of who else is teaching your topic, it's time to dig in and understand what they offer to their audiences, how large their audiences are, what products they sell, what their values and priorities are, and so on. Most of this is readily apparent on their websites. From there, what's needed is for you to reach out to them. I will cover all this in more detail later in the book.

Your goal in working with promotional partners is always to have an opportunity to share your information with their audiences. You want them to interview you on a teleseminar or conduct a webinar with you, promote an online report or video you have posted, or direct their people to your blog posting. You want them to give you exposure. The second end goal you want is to turn that exposure into income by offering that audience something for sale. This is called affiliate marketing, which we will get into later in the book.

As a final note, there is a reason this step follows the others in our 10 steps. Do not go out there and try to get people to promote your message unless you have successfully done the previous eight steps. It is madness to ask someone to promote you if you don't know your topic, audience, and story or if you don't yet have a product, website, or campaign sequence created and tested. Frankly, until you have done those things, you wouldn't *want* someone to promote you even if they offered. I actually have several clients who have been on Oprah and who are, quite literally, broke. They got their fifteen minutes of fame with the best promotional partner in history, but they didn't have the back-end infrastructure up and running to monetize the attention. This happens all the time. Consider yourself warned, and don't let it happen to you. Build something real first; then ask others to help build it bigger. We'll cover more on partnering in coming chapters. For now, just realize it is *critical* to start searching for promotional partners, so be sure to complete the signposts below.

Expert Signposts:

1. Other experts training on my topic include...[I strongly suggest making a spreadsheet with all this information]

2. The audience size they have on Twitter and Facebook is...

3. The products they offer for sale on their website include...

4. The price points they most often offer to their audience are...

5. The values this person seems to live by are...

6. The common phrases this person uses are...

7. This person's priorities seem to include...

8. The information I have that their audience would likely value is...

Step 10: Repeat and Build the Business Based on Distinction, Excellence, and Service

None of these steps is a one-time affair. You will always be deepening your understanding of your topic and audience, creating new products, updating your websites, building campaigns, and getting new promotional partners. That is the work of being a Millionaire Messenger.

Throughout it all, I'd like you to keep in mind three values that have served me tremendously in our industry and helped me share my message with millions.

Value #1: Distinction

The first value is *distinction,* being unique. If you are always mindful about being your unique self and delivering unique value and content to your customers, you will meet the kind of success others dream of. Life, and our industry, does not reward cookie cutters or copycats. The better you get at being yourself and displaying your uniqueness to your fans and followers, the more influential you will become.

At a content level, I believe distinction to be my greatest asset. It is probably because my dad's advice on any topic almost always included "Just be yourself." I have taken this advice to the nth degree in business and become very strategic and purposeful about this. Because I have done my homework on all my peers and all the information and programs available to my customers, I know *exactly* how I am different and how my content is different. This allows me to be very persuasive in all my marketing—"*Hey, guys, choose my program because it is more this and less of that and specifically it will help you x."* I share this with you because I believe it is absolutely critical to your long-term success to keep an eye on the industry and best practices continually so that you know how your content and information measure up to the rest of the offerings in the marketplace.

Value #2: Excellence

The second value I encourage you to make part of your expert empire is *excellence.* Standing out in any role, career, or industry is simple if you are driven by excellence more than your counterparts are. To me, excellence is about giving your greatest effort and caring enough about your career and customers to make sure the value you bring is equal to or better than anything else out there. It is about striving to be a master and leader in what you do.

I often coach my clients to consider that excellence in our industry is 360 degrees—we have to require excellence of ourselves, our staff, and even our customers.

In our own work, we must continually push ourselves to improve. It's easy not to do this, because as messengers we often find ourselves surrounded by committed fans and followers. So it is easy to start resting, to stop pushing our limits, and to stop delivering everything we do with greater and greater levels of excellence. But the masters in this community are always pushing themselves to be better writers, speakers, facilitators, coaches, marketers, businesspeople, leaders, and servants. They are driven by a hunger to grow and contribute and be the best at what they do. And they know this benefits their brand and business. As my friend Paula Abdul said when she dropped in and surprised my audience at Experts Academy, "There's no traffic beyond the extra mile."

With our staff and contractors, we have to be the ambassadors of excellence. We have to lead them in such a way that they develop an obsessive focus on being the best at what they do. This might sound obvious, but most experts and entrepreneurs do not consider their work a real business, so they miss this critical aspect of being a successful business.

We also have to challenge our customers to be their best in everything we teach them to do. The sad truth is that most people do not have someone in their lives to push them to grow as a person and become better at what they do. So *be that person* for your customers. Challenge them to be their best selves and act with excellence. It is amazing what happens when you do that. Suddenly people start seeing you as their coach, and they are more likely to become fans and lifelong customers. They say to themselves, "Wow, this expert is pushing me to be my highest self, and she is showing me the path to growth and excellence. I'm a fan." The more you set accountability and the standard of excellence for people, the more they become attached to your work and the value you are providing—because nobody else is doing that for them.

Value #3: Service

The foundation of what we do in the expert industry is serving others. I love that our business is based on helping others by providing valuable information that can improve their lives. This really is your job from now on.

I think of the value of service in two ways. First, it means approaching this work from a place of service in your heart and mind. The entrepreneurial experts who ascend to making millions of dollars and reaching millions of people, those who become Millionaire Messengers, get in this business and stay in this business for the right reasons. They care about helping others. They have a deep connection with those they serve. They genuinely want to help others solve their problems and reach their potential. They create great products and information not because doing so will make them millionaires but because it will help improve millions of lives.

Every Millionaire Messenger I've ever met is driven by empathy, compassion, and altruism. Their friends and family say they have a huge heart, and many in their community call them "do-gooders." It's as if they are so connected to the idea of helping others with what they know that if you took away their business of doing so, they would be completely lost. Messengers see their work as most others view volunteerism: as an opportunity to give from the heart. They are servant leaders.

This value of service doesn't just mean doing things for the right reasons. It also means doing things right when it comes to customer service. Our industry needs to take better care of its customers and approach customer service even more seriously than Fortune 500 companies do. We need to deliver what is promised, have people available to respond to e-mails and calls within the same day, stand by our guarantees, and seek to deliver our customers consistently great value. These ideas apply to any business. But the nature of our work compels us to pay even more attention to customer service excellence. Your name is often your business in this industry—think "Tony Robbins." If you don't take care of your customers, word quickly spreads. Your name, your brand, and your entire business can be quickly destroyed if you don't take good care of your customers. And for whatever reason, mistreated customers in our industry take to the Web to express their disenchantment more than in other sectors of the economy. "Guru bashing" is a common phrase, and that language alone lets you know that people do enjoy going after experts and gurus in any field. It's just one more reason why you always have to take care of your customers.

Expert Signposts:

1. What makes me distinct in this industry is that I...

2. The reason I am committed to being excellent in everything I do is...

3. The reason I am doing this work in the first place is to...

The purpose of this chapter was to give you a big-picture overview of your new career. Follow these 10 steps repeatedly and you will begin building a great expert empire. In the next chapter, we'll see where the rubber hits the road and where the money comes from in this industry. You'll learn how entrepreneurial experts often become Millionaire Messengers through five simple programs. Before moving on, be sure to do your "homework" and do all the Expert Signpost exercises.

Chapter Six

THE MILLIONAIRE
MESSENGER'S MONEY MAP

Whenever I tell people that they can make a difference and an income at the same time by sharing their life story and advice with others, they often look at me as if I'd lost my mind. Many look at me as if to say, "Sure, man. Show me the money—where do all these dollars come from that these 'millionaire messengers' make?"

I've gotten that look enough to know it's important for me to talk money with you. I'll do that in this chapter, but let me make a few points before diving into the dollars.

First, I'm a lot like many of my readers, and money plays second fiddle to meaning in my life. The truth is that I'm much more driven by sharing my message than by having enough cash to buy anything I want. I suppose that comes from the way I was raised. When I was young my parents, both working full-time, never earned more than $40,000 combined. We didn't have much when I was growing up, so I guess I have never had ambition for a lot of material wealth.

However, I have learned a very important lesson about money these past few years: *Money is a grand amplifier*. If you want to get your message out there in a big way and you want to sustain it, having more money makes that possible. It sounds odd to write that (for me), but after working with tens of thousands of entrepreneurial experts I know it to be true. You simply need to make money to continue sharing and sustaining your message.

That's why, in this chapter, I'm going to be blunt about money and how it's made in our industry. I don't want you to be another would-be author, speaker, coach, seminar leader, or online marketer whose message dies because you have to spend all your time doing unfulfilling side work that keeps you from your artistry and your message.

So let's get to it. How do experts make money? How could you make a million dollars without building a massive organization that chokes your entrepreneurial freedom? It's much, much simpler than you would ever have guessed.

The Six Profit Pillars for Entrepreneurial Experts

Entrepreneurial experts make money through one or more of the following activities:

- Writing
- Speaking
- Giving Seminars
- Coaching
- Consulting
- Online marketing

As authors, experts write their advice and how-to information and charge money for it. While writing a traditional book is the most common form of monetizing writing for experts, there are also other options. My clients and I have made money selling booklets (the shorter cousin to books, often 20 to 50 pages in length), eBooks (shorter electronic versions of books, often 20 to 50 pages in length), instructor guides (train-the-trainer manuals on my topics), membership site blogs (which people paid a subscription fee to read and could access with a unique login and password), article series (for other experts to license), and monthly subscription newsletters (delivered in print to my customers' homes once a month for a fee).

As speakers, experts make money by delivering presentations on their topic in one of three formats. First, they may market themselves as keynote speakers, charging organizations a speaking fee for what is typically a 30- to 90-minute speech. When speaking for longer durations, from two hours to two days, speakers take on the role of trainer and deliver their information for organizations in a much more detailed manner. Last—and this has become wildly popular and profitable in the past decade—speakers earn an income doing "platform sales," meaning they speak on promoters' stages and offer their higher-priced products and programs for sale directly to the audience from the stage. Basically, they teach their topic for 80 minutes or so and then, in the last 10 to 15 minutes, offer their programs for sale to the audience. In this format, "platform presenters" do not earn a fee to speak— they make money only if the audience buys their programs. In this case, the speaker splits the revenue 50–50 with the promoter. In today's world, many speakers also make a lot of money releasing video training online, but I'll reserve that discussion for later.

As seminar leaders, experts host their own live events. I simply group all these live training events under "seminars," but they are often described as workshops, conferences, educational retreats, training intensives, transformational weekends, and so on. Seminars, as I will argue later, are often the most lucrative pillars of profit for entrepreneurial experts. They are also one of the greatest positioning efforts an expert can do—if you have a live seminar on your topic, then many people will see you as a leading authority on the topic (and many other speakers on your topic will also want to speak on your stage).

As life and business coaches, experts make money by charging clients for individual or group coaching sessions. The most common form of coaching is similar to the therapeutic model—clients pay coaches by the hour for their advice. This often involves a life coach talking with customers in person or over the phone for one hour a week or a month. In the more scalable and lucrative group-coaching model, a coach may host weekly or monthly coaching calls with a group of clients, teaching for part of the call and then conducting question-and-answer sessions.

As consultants, experts make money by charging organizations, usually by the hour or by the completed project, for their actual services in creating, collaborating on, and completing a specific project. In the new world economy, this is often the most labor-intensive approach at making money as an expert. You have to find organizational clients, pitch them your services, and then work individually or with your team to deliver them. I personally seldom recommend this model for my experts, because of the time and scalability challenges. It is very hard to scale a coaching model without building a larger employee-based team, but many have done this successfully, so I include it here. Depending on your goals, consulting can be a great option, especially if you love solving larger organizational challenges. Disclosure: I was a high-paid consultant for the world's largest consulting company for six years of my life, so perhaps I just grew tired of the hours, pressure, and politics.

Finally, as online marketers, experts make money by packaging their advice and how-to knowledge into informational products and programs that people purchase online. This is the new "Promised Land" of experts and all entrepreneurs. The Internet has decimated old distribution conventions and allowed us to capture directly, communicate with, and sell to our customers. Experts now commonly offer their content and how-to training through webinars, software, membership sites, downloadable audio and video programs, monthly content releases, desktop training programs, and so much more. Today's experts are essentially online retailers of information. And unlike with our brick-and-mortar counterparts, business is booming. Setting up a website to add value to customers, capture leads, and deliver content for a fee is easier and faster than ever. At Experts Academy, we've shown and proved how entrepreneurial experts can be up and running online in less than a single day. It's incredible.

The nice part about all these roles—author, speaker, seminar leader, coach, consultant, and online marketer—is that you get to choose which best matches your style and lifestyle preferences. Are you an awesome writer who doesn't want to travel? Then being an author and online marketer makes a lot of sense. Love the stage, lights, and traveling to new cities? Then becoming a speaker and seminar leader could be a blast. Would you rather work one-on-one with clients or hang your shingle out as a coach or consultant?

While choice is wonderful, you also don't necessarily have to choose. Most experts, at least those of us who are building seven-figure businesses, wear many of these hats as part of our business strategy. The truth is that if you only wear one of these hats, you are essentially limited in your income, and you are in danger of not creating a real business.

Here's a common example. Many of the people who attend Experts Academy have been *New York Times* best-selling authors. You would think they were beyond wealthy and famous. But many are unknown and broke. How can that be possible? Because though they had a best-selling book, there was nothing beyond the book—they didn't have a great website or other products and services available for sale. When their 15 minutes of fame had elapsed, their new fans had nothing else to purchase. This is so common that it's frightening, and I would surmise that our industry, especially the book industry, rivals the music industry in the number of one-hit wonders.

To truly evolve and expand as an expert, you'll want to begin cultivating all six areas into a multiple-streams-of-revenue business model. You don't have to, but trust me, you'll want to once you see the impact, influence, and income you can generate when you mix writing, speaking, leading seminars, coaching, consulting, and online marketing.

I'm a best-selling author, an in-demand speaker, a seminar leader who sells out every event, a coach with a long waiting list of $25,000-per-year clients, a consultant who picks and chooses projects, and an online marketer whose products make millions. Now, here's the kicker: I do all this with a minimal staff and a very simple business model.

This last point is worth repeating. As an entrepreneurial expert, you do not need a large staff, if any at all. As you will recall, I made my first million without a single employee. How is that possible? It's possible because, in most cases, all you need for infrastructure in this business are a phone, a laptop, and a message. From there, everything is positioning, packaging, promoting, and partnering with others to get your message out there. I'll cover these four P's in Chapter Eight, "The Millionaire Mandates."

A Million-Dollar Expert Empire in Five Steps

Let me show you how all these roles and profit pillars can come together to create a very simple plan for building a million-dollar expert business.

This plan was created for Sally, one of my $25,000-per-year clients, who asked me once, quite bluntly, "Brendon, I need a plan to make a million dollars in twelve months, and I want to be able to do it without building a huge infrastructure or hoping for the luck to stumble onto tens of thousands of new clients."

In almost every industry, this would be quite a challenging problem. In the expert industry, it's fairly straightforward. In fact, I showed this client that she could accomplish her goal with just hundreds of customers, with no staff, and with just the following six basic work efforts.

1. Create a low-priced information product

First, I told Sally to create a lower-priced information product. Of course, she said, "What's that?" I'm sure you have the same question, so I will be defining my terms as we move through this plan.

In the expert industry, "low-price" is typically anything in the $20–$200 range. An "information product" is basically training material—your advice or strategies for success packaged into an educational product or program. In this price range, an information product is often a book, eBook, CD audio program, or DVD home-study course.

Let's assume Sally creates an audio program consisting of just seven CDs and that sells for $197. An audio program like this is easy to create. Sally just needs to buy a decent microphone and plug it into her computer, and with the free software on her computer she can record her voice and training. All she needs to do is record seven one-hour sessions, which ultimately become the seven CDs in her audio program. Once she has the MP3 files from her recordings, she can send them to a CD manufacturer and have them create her CDs and product design. Bam! Sally has a product, which the manufacturer prints on demand and fulfills. Now all Sally needs is a website to sell the program.

Now let's get to the numbers. If Sally sells just one program a day at $197 in a 30-day month, she would earn $5,910 a month. Multiply that amount by 12 months, and this product can make her $70,920 a year. Not bad. She made $70,000 a year and only needed 365 customers to do it. But this is just the beginning.

At this point, let me address the ignorance of skeptics. Many newbies or outside observers would say, "Oh, my God, who would ever pay $197 for an audio program when you can get books on tape for $10?" What these types of questions display is a general lack of understanding about the expert industry. The value of any given program in our industry is not how much it *costs* to create but how much *value* it delivers. Expertise is not a commodity like toothpaste. For example, a seven-disk audio program can generally be manufactured and fulfilled for around $15–$25, but it's certainly worth more than that if it solves someone's problems or improves someone's life or business, right? As an example, my friend Tony Robbins sells a wonderful personal development audio program called "Get the

Edge." It's just seven CDs in a nice box. I bought it for around $297 a few years ago, and it changed my life. Is a life change worth $297? I think so. Anyone who doesn't is simply not my customer or yours.

Let's move on and see how the dollars start adding up.

2. Create a low-priced subscription program.

So now we have Sally up to $70,920 a year just by selling a $197 audio program. On top of this, I suggested she create a subscription program, which, in the expert community, is often called a membership program or continuity program. Just like the magazine business model, a subscription program in the expert industry is based on delivering monthly content to your customers.

In this step, I suggested Sally create a monthly program where she sent customers a new training video every month. I also suggested she host a monthly training call over a conference call line in which she gave more training and answered questions as well. To access the video and the call replays, her customers could log in to a members-only site and download the video and audio recordings.

At a low-tier price point in our industry, Sally can charge from $9.97 all the way up to $197 a month for her training, based on her positioning and the value delivered to her clients. I suggested we start her at the $97 subscription point.

Looking at the numbers, if Sally gets just 100 people to pay $97 a month for her subscription program, she would be earning an extra $9,700 per month, which equals an astounding $116,000 per year.

Imagine making $116,000 a year with just 100 clients, and all you have to do is send out a video and host a call once a month. In the expert industry, it happens all the time.

Now, keep in mind that you don't have to do a video and conference call every month. You could simply send out a specialty newsletter or new audio CD every month. You don't even have to personally create the content or products yourself. You could hire a freelancer to write the articles or create training videos, or you could partner with other experts to send their content out to your customers. The options are endless, and you get to pick which modality you like to work in the most.

I hope I don't have to remind you that this is all based on your delivering excellent value and content to your customers. But do you see how fast this all adds up?

Let's keep stacking services on our way to $1,000,000.

3. Create a mid-tier-priced information product.

Next, I asked Sally to consider making a more advanced and comprehensive training program that could be sold at the mid-tier price point. For reference, a low-tier price point is around $10–$200; a mid-tier price point is usually $200–$999; and a high-tier is $1,000 and above.

The low- to high-tiering structure is for illustration purposes only. The reality is that mid-tier for personal development is different than for real estate or programs on building wealth, and so on. For example, a $497 product is considered high-tier in the personal development space, but "cheap" and low-tier in the online marketing space.

Let's say Sally created a $497 DVD home-study course on her topic, which she mailed to people's houses. The home-study course could include 10 DVDs, transcripts, a workbook, and a bonus 3-disk audio program. If she sold 60 units a month, just two a day, that would equal $29,820 a month, which adds up to a whopping $357,840 a year.

Notice that I'm not asking Sally to sell tens of thousands of units here. We are talking about just 60 customers a month in this example, and she then earns $357,840 a year with just this one product. The average American earns less than $65,000, so this is incredible by most people's standards.

But we're just getting warmed up. Because all those people whose lives have been transformed by Sally's audio, subscription, and DVD programs will want to see her live one day, they will want to go to her seminar.

4. Create a high-tier multiday seminar.

Running seminars is the most lucrative empire-building strategy for experts that I know. Think about any "guru" you've ever followed. Did they have a seminar or live event workshop? Of course they did. What's interesting is that they probably didn't start their seminars because they wanted to be a seminar leader someday. Instead, they started them because their customers *demanded* it. The reality is that customers in our industry are interested in mastery, in continuing their education. So if they have bought your book and audio and DVD programs, they now want to go deeper and learn from you live. It's not unlike the music industry—customers buy CDs but at some point yearn for the live concert.

Oddly, most experts are terrified of doing their own seminars. But again, most fear is due to uncertainty—their lack of knowledge in how to conduct seminars creates a lack of confidence. Seminars actually happen to be very easy and lucrative to pull off if you know what you're doing, and you don't need thousands of people in a room to succeed.

For example, in the next 12 months do you think you could get just 100 people into a conference room to learn from you? I bet you could if you positioned, packaged, promoted, and partnered well.

Let's imagine that Sally plans all year and gets just 100 people into her seminar, each one paying $1,000 to attend. They pay that amount because it is Sally live and in person; it is also her best content. She has brought in a few other experts as guest speakers, and the seminar is held at a nice resort that's easy to reach by airplane. If you can't persuade 100 people to come to a seminar, and you have 12 entire months to do so, then you've probably lost all ability to communicate. Think about it: You would only have to get nine or so people a month to sign up over those 12 months to put 100 in a room.

Playing out the numbers on this example, Sally would earn $100,000 in ticket sales. That's just for one weekend of training, and it includes only the ticket sales. We're not even counting the "back-end" sales: the additional product and program purchases that customers make at the live event. The back end of a seminar is often worth twice the front end, but just to keep things simple while illustrating our million-dollar plan, we won't even include that number here.

In the first seminar I ever did, I had around 28 people in a room paying twice that: $2,000. And I didn't know half as much as you do now about this industry. I couldn't believe it. I had made $56,000 in one weekend. The total costs to host the event were just $5,000, which included the room and presentation screen rental. I remember it fondly because I had to do everything myself. back then, I didn't have a team to video the program or run the lights and music. I borrowed a projector from a friend and brought snacks for the attendees. I ran the entire event off my laptop, which sat on a tiny table with a long skirt. I bought some cheap computer speakers and put them underneath the table. Before and after breaks, I would put some music on, talk to customers, get everyone dancing, and then turn the music off myself. It was hilarious from a production standpoint, but the program changed people's lives. We all start somewhere. These days our seminars are a bit fancier, and we regularly fill a room with hundreds of people paying $3,495 to $5,000 per ticket.

Back to our example: Sally has just made $100,000 at her first seminar, on the front end only. She will soon find that people want to go even deeper with her training and request her personal coaching.

5.   Create a high-priced coaching program.

When Sally's fans and customers want to get her personal attention and continuing education at the mastery level, they will want to hire her as a life/business coach.

There are many ways to create a coaching program, and we teach them all at Experts Academy. One would be for Sally to be hired as a traditional one-on-one life coach or business coach. In this role, she would assess her clients' needs and work with them to discover where they are and where they want to go. Then she would create a plan to move the clients closer toward their dream, and she would begin coaching each client to implement that plan, stay accountable, and grow as a person or professional. Most of the coaching and conversations happen over the phone. Although any professional coach will tell you there is really more to it than this—and they would be right—this is a broad overview of the business.

Pricing in the coaching business has become more and more of a crapshoot these days. As an industry, the average life coach likely earns between $150 and $350 per hour. But that's the average, and being average will not make you a millionaire. I rarely recommend that people focus solely on individual and "traditional" life or business coaching, because it's simply not scalable. You can coach only so many people in the traditional hourly model. And even if you kept your calendar packed with coaching calls and live meetings, you would face the same issue that therapists, doctors, lawyers, and other hourly professionals ultimately deal with: You'd start hating your life.

I experienced this personally, too. I remember having so many coaching clients at one point that I started to dread being on the phone all day. My life became all about the clock and the calendar, and that is no way for an entrepreneur to live.

The best model for scaling a coaching practice is to start doing group coaching, so let's use that as an example here. Let's say Sally creates a high-end $2,000-per-month group coaching program. In this program, Sally's customers get exclusive new training videos every month, a group training and question-and-answer conference call, two free tickets to her live seminar, and a separate live weekend event each year for coaching clients only. She might talk to her group members individually once a month, or she might not. If she were my client, I would recommend not. The value the group gets is the exclusive training and access with both Sally and the group. I love this model, and many in our community have been very successful with it.

If Sally gets just fifteen people into this $2,000-a-month program, it equates to $30,000 a month and $360,000 per year.

With this last strategy in place, we have created an entirely new million-dollar expert empire from scratch for Sally by doing just five things. Let's look at how all these numbers add up.

1. If Sally sells just one low-priced audio program a day at $197, she will earn $5,910 a month, or $70,920 a year.
2. If Sally sells just 100 people into a $97-a-month subscription program, she will earn $9,700 a month, or $116,400 a year.
3. If Sally sells just 60 mid-tier products a month at $497, she will earn $29,820 a month, or $357,840 a year.
4. If Sally sells just 100 seminar tickets at $1,000, she will earn another $100,000 a year.
5. If Sally sells just 15 coaching clients at $2,000 a month, she will earn $30,000 a month, or $360,000 a year.

Combined, these five strategies earn Sally $1,005,160 a year!

What's remarkable about this plan is that it doesn't require Sally to have dozens upon dozens of products, or thousands upon thousands of clients. She needs just five programs for people to enroll in. To become a millionaire, she needs to sell just one low-priced audio program a day, 100 subscriptions at $97 a month, 60 mid-tier products a month, 100 seminar tickets over the course of the year, and 15 coaching clients.

Of course, this is just a sample plan, and there are plenty of ways to reach a million dollars. Sally could decide to focus solely on conducting seminars and make a million dollars selling 500 people a $2,000 ticket, or 2,000 people a $500 ticket. Or she could work exclusively on building a subscription/membership program and get 1,000 people paying her $97 a month to reach her million. Or she could sell 2,000 or so products at the $497 level, or sign up 45 coaching clients at $2,000 per month for a cool $1,080,000. Again, the possibilities are endless.

Right about here, many people raise objections to all this. They say, "Well, Brendon, not everyone can be an expert and do this." To this I reply, "Why not?" What is it about this industry that makes people think they can't do it? Clearly, anyone can learn and master a topic, right? And anyone can organize that knowledge into helpful advice, right? And these days anyone can put up a website and offer their programs for sale, right? So what's all the mystery about? I hope this book helps in debunking this myth.

Of course, it's certainly true that not everyone will become a millionaire or achieve extraordinary financial results. My aim here is not to guarantee that everyone will. I'm often asked, "Brendon, your example for making millions is great, but can anyone make money and become rich doing this?" As a legal disclaimer, I must say that my results are not typical and that no one is guaranteed to earn an income by following my (or anyone's) advice or strategies. I personally do not think anyone is guaranteed anything in life. Agreed? Besides, it's illegal to guarantee anyone results with your teaching, period. The law stems from the Federal Trade Commission in the United States, which, thankfully, prevents hucksters from making wild claims such as "Everyone who buys my course will become a millionaire overnight by buying foreclosed homes." The truth is that we all have different levels of ambition, knowledge, skill, talent, ability, resources, and commitment, so of course we are all going to get different results in life. That makes sense to me.

My goal in illustrating this simple plan is to show an example of how just a few product offerings can add up to a big opportunity. I'm just helping illuminate where all the money comes from in our industry so that it's no longer a mystery to beginners. I hope it serves to enrich your understanding of the industry and how it works.

Another objection we often hear relates to the numbers I used in my illustration. Many newbies and skeptics ask, "But some of those prices are so high! Who in the world are you to charge that much?" Well, who is *anyone* to charge money for anything? What gives any professional the right to charge any amount of money for anything? It's a concept called capitalism. It's supply and demand and the notion of an equal exchange of value. In our expert world, we know we can charge these amounts because, frankly, people pay them. Consumers vote with their wallets. If they didn't believe we were worth it, they would not pay the price we are asking. It's as simple as that.

Never forget that people pay a lot of money to shorten their learning curve and their path to success. Look at the exorbitant sums people are paying for college these days. Some would say it's atrocious. But people pay the tuitions, and they will continue to do so because learning is and always will be important. In the expert space, we take education to the next level by synthesizing and systemizing specific information that helps people solve their problems, whether personal or professional, and move ahead faster in life.

Luckily for us, demand is always high, and the world is always hungry for new strategies and ideas. To illustrate this point, consider the fact that while almost every sector of the economy was downsizing in the past few years, businesses run by well-rounded experts who live by the principles in this book saw extraordinary growth. Why? Because now more than ever millions of people are looking for inspiration and instruction to help them get ahead and stay motivated. People have been laid off in great numbers, the baby boomers are retiring, and a new generation is looking to succeed. All this bodes well for the entrepreneurial expert.

Here's the thing. If you personally do not think you can charge high prices, you're probably right. I've always believed that a person's potential is limited only by their belief in themselves and what is possible. If your beliefs stop you from believing that you and your information and expertise are valuable, then no one can help you. No one will ever show up at your door with a certification that says, "Congratulations! You are now qualified to raise your prices!" As with all things in life, the way to get something you want, including getting to the point where you can charge good money for your good advice, rests on how hard you will work and how much value you add. Not everyone will work hard, add equal value, or succeed.

Personally, I *do* have an opinion about who succeeds in building wealth in this business and who doesn't. And I do think it's rather predictable. To many of my students' surprise, I don't think it comes down to how smart you are, how well connected you are, how attractive you are, or how wealthy you are. I also don't think it comes down to having the perfect business plan or website. It's also not about how big a subscription list you have.

I believe it's more about what Tony Robbins often says: "It's not about your resources, it's about your resourcefulness." I didn't have a lot of business knowledge, connections, or money when I began, as I have already shared with you. I also didn't have a plan, a website, or a list. Many of my clients start the same way—with nothing but a dream and a desire to help others.

What successful experts do have in common is that they have the right *mind-set* and *mandates* to follow. In other words, we have the right psychology and set of practices that helped us start out and grow a real business. In the next two chapters, we'll cover these two areas in detail.

A Reminder

As we move from our discussion of money to mind-set, let's get back to the heart of why we do this important work. You clearly have the chance to earn an extraordinary income being an expert. Out of necessity, I had to teach you to make money because I know that it's required for you to start out and sustain your message. The more money you make, the more you can spread your message. But with all the focus on making money and running the business, it can be easy to get away from why we do what we do. We always have to remind ourselves that despite the immensity of the financial opportunity we have in the expert space, we have an even greater calling and obligation to serve. Our mission is to improve the lives and businesses of those we serve, by providing great value and information.

Just like any other entrepreneur, experts can quickly succumb to focusing on the financial and operational side of the business. It's easy to lose the meaning of what we do when we have to deal with money and hard-to-please customers. And now that we all do so much work virtually and can serve the masses through the Web, we often lose the connection with our individual customers. It is that personal connection that reminds us of just how great a difference our work makes.

I've experienced this personally. Between the travel I do for speeches and seminars, the isolation I force on myself to write new articles and books, and the hurry I make to get the latest new video or promotion finished and posted on the Web, I've sometimes felt more stress than satisfaction. There are days when I don't speak with a single customer, and others when I correspond with some I'd rather not have. There are days when my staff lets me down or I let them down. There are days that I want to throw my computer out the window. And there are plenty of days when I feel alone in this industry because we rarely all get together to create a real community.

I think that's part and parcel of any entrepreneurial effort. But I never lose sight of why I'm doing what I do, and it's vitally important to remind yourself of that often in this business. If you always keep in mind the fact that your work is changing lives, you will stay motivated, do the right things, and take care of your customers. And if you do a good job and keep the lines of communication open with your customers, they will remind you as well of why you do what you do.

I remember one particularly busy time in my expert business that taught me a great lesson. I was becoming more and more recognized for my work, so I was getting a lot of new opportunities. In a six-month period, I had hired two new contractors, created four new websites, started two new seminars, made a million dollars, traveled to dozens of cities, launched a new online training program, and moved my mother from her home in Montana to Las Vegas following the death of my father. I was burned out, exhausted. We had a thousand new issues we never faced before, and as we grew, we started to get a few customers who really took advantage of our generosity. Many people were stealing our content or illegally copying it and selling it. The money was pouring in. I was so busy, though, that I didn't feel much excitement, because I was starting to lose touch with the magic of what we do.

And then I received an e-mail from a customer who was touched by *Life's Golden Ticket*. I'll end this chapter with it because it reminds us all of how meaningful our work can be. A world away, someone found importance in my work. In all our insanity and hurry, we sometimes forget how much our work helps and inspires others, even when we don't always see it or hear about it. I receive thousands of e-mails of thanks each month, but this one stopped me cold and truly made me thankful. Do good work in the world and put your message out there. Even when you don't know you're making a difference, you are.

[This is an actual e-mail I received. It has been edited only to protect the sender's privacy.]

Brendon, you don't know me, just another name on your list. Don't worry I'm not some nut job or stalker or someone looking to sell you anything.

A few months back I received your book. I was inspired by your story and attitude, I really admired what you were saying. It had a profound effect on me. I have shared the book with some close friends, whom I thought could benefit from the in sight

Three weeks ago, on a drive up to a family wedding in the country, I talked to my wife about the book, whilst our kids slept in the back. She is one of those who never engages in my "work" bits, but she too was moved by your story, and she asked to read the book when we got back.

We had a great time at the wedding. On the way home from the wedding, however, we were involved in a traffic accident, and were hit head on by a vehicle heading the wrong way down the carriage way, my wife was killed instantly, my daughter died the next day from severe brain trauma.

As I lay there in hospital. I kept thinking of your story, and it gave me hope. I tried to write you in the hospital, but couldn't control my tears.

I just wanted to say thank you for sharing your story with me, it helped me cope,

I'm still raw and don't know what will come next, but thanks.

Chapter Seven

THE MESSENGER MIND-SET

What makes the Millionaire Messenger successful? What does it take to succeed in the expert industry?

I'm asked these questions at every Experts Academy event and on every interview I do on the topic. These are not easy questions to answer, and I highly encourage you to sit down and answer them yourself. What do you think it will take to start out and win?

To answer these questions for myself has taken years of interviewing industry legends and practicing what I've learned. What I've found, like so many before me, is that most success in life is an internal game. It's usually more about how you think, feel, and behave than the tools or resources you have at hand. Your psychology and practices are more important than anything, and that is why I've chosen to address them in this and the next chapter.

I believe that successful experts have four dominant beliefs that allow them to consistently serve, share, work, and create. With these four beliefs running their mind and their life, they are driven to make a real difference and build a real business. Without these four beliefs, would-be experts give up early, lose focus, fail—or, worse, they never begin.

Mind-set #1: My life experience, message, and voice are valuable.

Psychologists long ago discovered that a person's happiness, efficacy, and ability to be resilient and both emotionally and socially intelligent all hinge on a their evaluation of their *worth*. In fact, many believe that self-worth is the foundation on which we form most of our thoughts, feelings, and behaviors. Pioneers in the self-esteem movement, including leading theorist Nathaniel Branden, tell us that self-worth is the key to understanding and cultivating self-esteem and success in life. It is a proven equation in psychology: The worthier you feel, the more capable and confident you feel.

The same, of course, is true in our industry. If you don't value *who you are and what you have to say*—your life experience, message, and voice—then you will never have a shot at feeling or becoming confident and successful as an expert. If *you* don't value your voice, who else will?

I could write volumes on how many great people have let their great advice for others die quietly in a journal somewhere because they thought, "Well, who on earth *cares* what I think?" Or, worse, "*Who am I* to share what I think with others?" I know of no greater indicator of low self-esteem and self-worth than the phrase *Who am I to...*

This is not to say that all Millionaire Messengers always have rock-solid self-esteem or profoundly positive senses of self or ego. In fact, I have met many experts who actually lack the personal self-confidence you would think they had. But here's what makes them different from others:

They have a hunger to share and serve.

And it is that hunger—a deep-down psychological need and desire—to share and serve others with what they know that forms the expert's belief that their message and voice are valuable.

Where does that hunger come from? You might be surprised by the answer.

Many observers of our community believe that the "gurus" all have a massive ego that drives them. Surely, they share their message to become rich, rewarded, and recognized, right? It's interesting that many unsuccessful or jealous people think that of others who are more successful, no matter the industry.

But after dozens of interviews and a few years at the top of this community, I can share this: The messenger's hunger to share their message doesn't come from ego; it comes from obligation. Yes, *obligation*.

While most people consider "obligation" a negative word—I used to, as well—it is astounding how many gurus use the word in a positive manner. They say, "Well, I experienced this big struggle or this traumatic event, and I consider the lessons I learned such a gift that I feel it is my obligation to share those lessons with others." Experts often use the term "moral obligation" or "calling" to describe this drive.

I can relate. At a very deep level, I feel that I was given a gift with life's golden ticket—my second chance at life—and that sharing what I learned is my duty, a calling, and an obligation. I value my life experience, my message, and my voice because I believe these things to have been a gift to me. And if God and the universe valued the experiences I have had in my life enough to give them to me, then I value them enough to pass them on to others.

Many of my clients feel the same way. A grief coach I know says she chose to be a coach because she met so many other people who were struggling with how to cope with the loss of a loved one that she felt a moral obligation to counsel them through the experience. A best-selling author told me that he started workshops for new writers because it took him 10 years of begging agents and publishers to get published, and he didn't want anyone else to have to go through that. A personal finance adviser says he went bankrupt as a young man and spent a decade trying to clean up his credit and couldn't stand the thought of others getting calls from "those bastards at the collection agencies." A mother said her whole family wept thousands of tears as they painfully cared for their autistic child and that there needed to be more education for parents like her. She said she felt "a light go on one day when we finally figured it out. I *must* tell other moms that they don't have to hate themselves or their children anymore, because there's a better way to parent autistic children."

I imagine that what you have been through in life has taught you a lot. The good times and the bad are important, and the lessons you have learned from both are profoundly valuable. There is no question that life has not always been easy for you. And I bet you haven't always been clear on why you had to endure the hardships and why you struggle so much for the successes. But let me make the same claim those who believe in mentorship have claimed for decades: If you have learned a valuable lesson in life or business, then it's your obligation to share that with others so they don't have to go through the same drama, struggle, or miles traveled to figure it out.

If you believe that, then it's all a matter of your following the steps I've laid out for you so far. It's time for you to act. You're going to change a lot of people's lives.

Expert Signposts:

1. One reason I have not been sharing my life lessons more with others is because...

2. If a friend of mine used an excuse like that reason, I would say to them...

3. The times in my life when I have held back my voice have been times like...

4. The times in my life when I spoke up and helped others include...

Mind-set #2: If I don't know it or have it, I will go learn it or create it.

Never doubt a person with a calling or moral obligation—they will find a way to share their message. That dedication is ingrained in the mind of every Millionaire Messenger I know. Regardless of what they don't know or don't have, they will *find a way* to share their message.

I never knew how critical this belief was in my life until I started marketing Experts Academy. As any good marketer does, I always listen for the objections and concerns my customers have that prevent them from buying my products and services. Remember, my Experts Academy is focused exclusively on authors, speakers, seminar leaders, coaches, and online marketers. To my utter surprise and disbelief, the strong objections people had about starting an expert empire included things like the following:

"But I don't know how to write a book."

"But I don't have an agent."

"But I don't know how to get hired as a speaker."

"But I don't have a demo DVD of me speaking."

"But I don't know how to conduct a seminar."

"But I don't have an event planner to help me."

"But I don't know how to get clients as a coach."

"But I don't have any coaching materials."

"But I don't know how to market my materials online."

"But I don't have a website."

When I tell you I was shocked at hearing these objections, I truly mean it. I would read people's e-mails and blog comments, see these types of statements, and think, "*What is wrong with these people?* One, that is what I'm offering to teach them. But two, no one knows or has these things to start with—they just go figure it out and GO!"

And thus began my great education on why many of the top entrepreneurial experts are so different. It turns out that we have a dominant belief that allows us to get ahead. That belief is that no matter what we know or have, we will start, struggle through, experiment, work hard, and learn or create whatever we must to get our message out there.

Empowered by this knowledge, I can now sit with someone for 10 minutes and know their fate as an expert and entrepreneur. If at any point they whine, "Well, I don't know this," or "I don't have that," then I know they will fail. It's not that they're saying they don't know or have what they need; it's often *how* they say it. If they sound weak, defeated, or unempowered, then I immediately know they don't stand a chance in this business. I also know, just by their tone, a lot about their lives.

Here's another powerful distinction I've learned: If you ever look at a successful person and say, "Well, sure, *they* could do it, but *I* can't," then you are defeated before you begin. You see, successful people had to start one day just like anyone else. If you have a mind-set that says successful people are blessed by the gods or luckier or more privileged than you are, then you are doomed. Instead, you might say, "Well, that person achieved this, so I can, too. I just have to model what they and others have done, and follow their lead."

Expert Signposts:

1. The things I'll have to learn in order to succeed in this new expert endeavor include…

2. The things I'll have to create in order to start include…

3. The people I can model and follow to shorten my learning curve include…

4. The excuses I'll probably make along the way, which I'll have to overcome, include…

Mind-set #3: I will not let my small business make me small-minded.

It's tough to start a new business venture, in this industry or any other. I like to tell entrepreneurs to prepare for the fact that the first two years in any business are scary, risky, draining, and frustrating.

Seriously, the first two years running your own business can be both horrible and the most exhilarating and fulfilling time in your life. You hope to quickly "make it big," but results almost always come more slowly than you anticipated. Still, you find the challenge, freedom, ownership, and connection with your customers meaningful and rewarding. I share this because it's always the first two years that stop newbies in our industry. They start out excited to share their message, but because the results can come in slowly, they give up their vision. It's easy to stop when your vision is not immediately mirrored in your bank account. It's easy to stop and play small in life when you aren't earning income at the rate and levels you hoped for.

But I have a message for you: Never let your small business make you small-minded.

Don't give up on your vision or play small just because you are starting out.

I remember how critical this belief was to me when I was just entering this industry. I still see myself sitting in a tiny apartment in San Francisco, broke because every dollar I had was going to rent and cheap burritos. I was writing on a tiny three-legged foldout table my mom used to use in her sewing room. I vividly recall a moment sitting there looking at my outdated laptop gather condensation on the screen as the broken radiator hissed out steam to warm the apartment. I was drafting a newsletter on the psychology of success—to be e-mailed to my unsuspecting friends, coworkers, and acquaintances—and I thought, "Who am I fooling? Who cares what a poor, goofy kid has to say about success?"

I also remember what my next thought was. I said, "Brendon, yes, you are starting out small, kid; everyone has to. But you have a powerful message, and you need to share it with others. You have studied this; you have learned a lot in life, and you can inspire others. You are going to help millions of people someday. Today is the day; you just keep working at it. You are bigger than this stupid apartment because your dreams have no boundaries."

To many, this might sound like a hokey story, but it's important. You need to have a grand vision for yourself and your message, *despite your present circumstances,* which will propel you into action and achievement. Never forget that all good results come slowly. While you are waiting for the big break to come, just keep in mind how important your work is and how many you will serve one day.

Even if you feel tethered to the ground of your current reality, set your sights high. Believe in your potential and a grand destiny for yourself. It will make those first steps more confident and sustain you when you stumble. I was inspired to believe this by Marianne Williamson, who has spoken at my events. Marianne is one of the greatest writers and teachers in our community. Her most famous quote from her book *A Return to Love* says it all:

"Our deepest fear is not that we are inadequate. Our deepest fear is that we are powerful beyond measure. It is our light, not our darkness, that most frightens us. We ask ourselves, Who am I to be brilliant, gorgeous, talented, fabulous? Actually, who are you not to be? You are a child of God. Your playing small does not serve the world. There is nothing enlightened about shrinking so that other people won't feel insecure around you. We are all meant to shine, as children do. We were born to make manifest the glory of God that is within us. It's not just in some of us; it's in everyone. And as we let our own light shine, we unconsciously give other people permission to do the same. As we are liberated from our own fear, our presence automatically liberates others."

Expert Signposts:

1. A grand vision I have for myself in this industry is to…

2. When times are tough I will always remind myself that…

3. To make sure I don't play small in life or in this business, I will…

4. To play a bigger game, I am going to have to let go of…

Mind-set #4: Student First, Teacher Second, Servant Always

All the experts I have ever met believe they are students and seekers at heart. They talk about all the books they read, and they seem to research hours on end, attend seminars, listen to tapes, and interview people. They pride themselves on their ability to learn and synthesize really good ideas that help people improve their lives or grow their businesses. Though they might not have an advanced degree, they are world-class students of life.

I think this is an important belief because many people who have given the word "expert" a bad name have done so by thinking they are "the one and only expert." These people, whom I would not even call experts, operate by ego rather than by calling, and they think they have figured everything out. They play a big game of positioning themselves as the "authority" on a matter, more out of personal pride and gain than out of any desire to serve. They stop learning, they stop collaborating with other communities of experts, and they ultimately lose touch with current best practices and, some might say, with reality.

To avoid this outcome, it's important that you always heed our mantra at Experts Academy: *Experts are students first, teachers second, servants always.*

If you have not read at least six books in the last six months on your topic of expertise, then you are not minding our mantra. If you have not tried to interview at least ten people on your topic this year, then you are not minding our mantra. If you are not actively scouring the Internet, researching journals, magazines, and bookshelves for information on your topic, then you are not minding our mantra. You are failing to be a student first. From this day forward, you must commit yourself to more disciplined and consistent study and mastery of your topic.

It is time to make life your own personal learning lab. You should start taking notes on little interactions you have as well as the big breakthroughs. Look for lessons in every moment and every relationship and record them in a journal. I remember learning the value of this from my journalism teacher in high school. Decades later, I would see it in practice with my friends Tony Robbins and Jack Canfield, two of the most diligent and productive note takers I have ever met in my life.

Millionaire Messengers have this interesting psychology that enables them to think of themselves as both student and teacher. They adopt the identity of world-class trainers. Like great educators, they are constantly trying to create strong and catchy teaching points, metaphors, frameworks, activities, and lesson plans that can help their students succeed. They carry around journals and take notes on what they see and learn about life that can empower others. To them, writing down new lessons and practicing new ways of teaching age-old wisdom is both a game and a career.

Personally, I'm almost obsessive about the practice of journaling new lessons to teach my audience. Every book I buy has countless notes in the margins reminding me of important concepts I can teach or make my own. I take copious notes at every seminar I attend, and always look for a unique teachable point of view. The identity of a teacher is a huge part of who I have decided to be in life. Ask anyone about me and they will tell you I'm always writing down new ideas and practicing new frameworks. Becoming an expert is not a one-time affair; it's a lifelong practice.

Finally, this all leads back to being a servant. It's almost impossible to dedicate yourself to a life of learning and teaching unless you have a *reason* to learn and teach. For most, that reason is to help others solve their problems and achieve their potential. It's vitally important to stay connected to the reason you are doing this work. In times of stress or frustration, your ultimate *why* for doing things is often the only thing that keeps you going.

Expert Signposts:

1. To feel more like a student in life, I would have to…

2. My plan for learning more about my topic is to…

3. My plan for capturing everyday life lessons that I can teach others is to start…

4. The reason I feel I should be learning all this and teaching what I know is…

Mind-set #5: Mastery is a way of life.

There are two types of people in the world. Both are blessed to enter a wide-open grand, green field of opportunity under which lie vast treasures. One type looks around the field, grabs the nearest shovel, and begins digging a hole in the ground, looking for gold. When this person gets a few shovels deep and discovers either (a) that they aren't hitting gold as fast as they thought they would, or (b) that there isn't as much gold as they thought, they stop digging and move to another random point in the field. They grab a newer, fancier shovel and start digging again, looking for gold. Again they find disappointment, so they move on and on and on. At the end of this person's life, their field of opportunity looks like a bunch of half-dug holes.

The other type approaches the field of opportunity differently. They scan the horizon and decide where they would like to stake their claim in life. They, too, begin digging for gold. They, too, may quickly discover either that (a) they are not hitting gold as fast as they thought they would, or (b) there is not as much gold as they thought. But here is where their fate unfolds differently than that of their unfocused peers: They keep digging. They think to themselves, "There is some gold here—maybe not as much as I thought or as easy to reach as I thought, but there is gold." They keep digging, working hard, staying focused. And soon enough, they hit the big payday, that vein of gold that is more abundant and awe-inspiring than they ever imagined. They set a foundation there—a fencepost of fortune, if you will. And then they move to another spot, aligned with their previous success, and they dig deep again, setting up another foundation and fencepost of wealth. At the end of this person's life, their field of opportunity looks like a line of strong foundations stretching into the sunset.

I often share this allegory at Experts Academy to remind people that a life of dabbling in dozens of topics or businesses often leads to failure, whereas a life of mastery leads to wealth.

In our industry it's tempting to try to be the "everything-under-the-sun expert," the person who knows about everything and does everything. That is why so many would-be experts fail. They get distracted. They start things in half measures, then give up too early and move on to a new thing and a new opportunity. Those who succeed, though, are the ones who choose to explore and master their topics deeply. They focus on one opportunity at once and dig deep, working for years to create a strong foundation. They understand the value of hard work, and they aren't afraid to put some blood, sweat, and tears into mining a worthwhile opportunity. They believe, often more than anyone else around them, that a life of dabbling is a life of distraction and a life of mastery is a life of meaning.

This emphasis on mastery helps you stay focused, overcome hardships, become a true expert in your field, and run a real business built on hard work and dedication.

Expert Signposts:

1. The topic area I am going to focus on like a laser for the next eighteen months is…

2. The things I am going to stop focusing on right now are…

3. The times when I lose my focus and fall off the path to mastery are usually when…

4. If, in twelve months, I looked back at my last year, I would know I had stayed on the path to mastery if I could see I had…

Chapter Eight

THE MILLIONAIRE MANDATES

The last chapter gave you the right psychology needed to share your message and build a real business while you are doing so.

If this is how experts think, I'm often asked, then what is it that they *do*? What do they excel at, and what do they consistently practice?

In many ways, the skill sets that experts must master relate specifically to the vehicle they choose to communicate their message through. Authors must develop writing skills. Speakers should develop presentation and persuasion skills. Seminar leaders should be great at facilitation; coaches should be excellent listeners and influencers, and so on.

Although this might seem obvious, our community has a decidedly disastrous perspective on skill development: It has none. Unlike other industries, our community has not embraced skill development, mostly because we have failed to view our calling as a real career choice.

In the corporate sector, employers and employees take skill development *very* seriously. Would-be employees evaluate potential employers based on how much training and skill development they will receive on the job. Companies invest billions of dollars and lots of personnel and talent in their human resource and organizational development departments to create elaborate "career paths," "fast-track" programs, and skill-building opportunities.

Oddly, though, our industry rarely talks about or focuses on skill development. One reason this sad reality exists is the convenient lie in our community that says, "You can just outsource everything and be the talent." That lie has cost thousands of up-and-coming experts thousands of wasted dollars and control over their fate. If you want to control your destiny in any career or industry, including ours, you need to develop real skill at what you are doing.

Coming from a corporate background, I attacked skill-building in this industry with zest and dedication, even when it was hard and boring. This has really set me apart and given me enormous control and confidence in my future.

Here's an example. In 2007, I realized that online video was going to be the dominant communication mode for experts in the future. Of course, 2007 seems late in the game to recognize this fact, but keep in mind that good, reliable, affordable technology did not yet exist for streaming longer-format video. The technology for shorter format did exist, but remember that experts deal in training, and our videos are often *an hour* or longer. At that time, very few people were effectively using video in online promotions or training programs.

Because of new streaming technologies that emerged around that time, it became possible to post training videos and webinar replays that were an hour or more long. This was a game changer. At the time, a small cadre of online marketing experts, including Frank Kern, Andy Jenkins, and Mike Koenigs, started waving the flag and telling our community to pay attention to using video in our marketing. But as of this writing, most experts are still not using video, even though it has proved to be more effective and lucrative for the industry. Why?

It's because few experts look to the horizon of our industry and ask, "What new skills will I need to develop to stay relevant, connected, and effective?" People ask that all the time in the corporate space, but not often in the entrepreneurial space.

In the case of online video, many leading experts thought, "Yes, video will be important someday. I'll just outsource it." It turns out that in the entrepreneurial world, "outsource" often equates to "I'll get around to it someday."

But I approached video very differently. I thought, "Video is becoming very important in our industry; therefore, it will be important to my long-term success in the industry. I had better learn it and develop skills, right now." With this in mind, I went to some free classes on shooting video being offered by a local art school. I researched shooting, editing, and posting videos. I e-mailed people who were using video in their online marketing, and asked how they did it.

Most importantly, I took action and bought a cheap Flip video camera and started shooting video in my apartment. My first videos were just me looking at the camera and teaching some basic personal development concepts. They were horrible. *Really* horrible. But the first time I rode a bike, it wasn't so pretty, either, and I approached video just like bike riding or any other skill—you get better with practice.

As of this writing, the way I'm using video online to market my expert empire is probably the most talked about in the industry. Using only video—sometimes direct to camera and sometimes using just screen-capture technologies to make a video recording of a Microsoft PowerPoint presentation—I have had remarkable success. In only twelve months, I used video exclusively in two million-dollar-plus promotions. I shoot on average one video per week, which adds massive value to my audience or coaching clients. Not bad for a kid who started with a Flip video camera.

The point here is not to impress you but to convey the importance of identifying a skill set that will be key to your long-term success, and to help you consistently and diligently develop that skill set. Video was important to my future, so I decided to master it. I have applied this same dedication to other skill areas that are important to my long-term success, including HTML coding, copywriting, product development, persuasion, and graphic design.

Heed my words: If it's important to your long-term success, don't outsource it—master it. Your success is powered by your skill sets.

In general, I say that everyone in our industry should develop skills in writing, specifically copywriting for marketing; speaking and persuasion; facilitating large groups; coaching individuals to achieve their goals; video shooting and editing; and blogging and social media. This might sound like a lot to learn, but I personally developed strong proficiency in each of these areas in under four years. Is four years worth a lifetime of confidence in your career? I would say so. The great benefit in our industry is that you are building most of these skills "on the job" as you promote your message anyway. To spread your message, you would do the following:

- Create a blog and a presence on social media websites.
- Write some posts and articles for your pages on those sites.
- Shoot, edit, and post videos on those sites.

In doing these things, you build your skills. By taking action, struggling through, figuring it out, asking lots of questions, and persisting, you suddenly have mastery.

Aside from the skills mentioned above, I believe that most highly paid experts focus most of their time on developing and practicing five broad skills that I call the "Messenger Mandates." These are unique skills you must develop to succeed in our unique industry. To call them "skills" is a bit of a misnomer, because they may be viewed as work efforts or tasks more than skill sets. However you slice it, the following five mandates are my response to the frequently asked question "To succeed in this industry, what do I need to be doing and what should I get really good at?"

Messenger Mandate #1: Positioning

Every expert must become skillful at what I call "positioning" in the industry. This is my big-bucket term for developing a good sense of (a) what your audience wants, and (b) what it takes to ensure that your customers and other experts in our community hold you and your content in high regard. If you are not well positioned in this industry, just as in any career or role, you cannot get ahead. You need to make sure you're talking to the right audience and that people notice you and quickly see your value vis-à-vis other players in your market space.

Let's start with positioning yourself well with your audience. It should go without saying that you need to know who your audience is and what they want. Once you have that knowledge, you need to deliver incredibly useful and actionable information to them on a regular basis. The less valuable and less frequent your contact with them, the "lower" you are positioned. If you're not at the top of their minds, you are not relevant or remembered. If you don't frequently hear this phrase from your audience, you're doing a horrible job of positioning yourself: "Wow, I can't wait to get your next [video, newsletter]! Whenever I see your name in my in-box, it's the first note I open!

You also have to position yourself purposefully vis-à-vis other experts. I know "positioning" is a weird term, so let me illustrate this concept. When I decided to start teaching personal development seminars, I started researching my "competitors." (I don't consider anyone a competitor in our community, since we are all unique.) I wanted to know who else was teaching my topics, what they were teaching, *how* they were teaching, how they marketed their programs, how much they charged, what their websites looked like, and so on. I subscribed to everyone's newsletters, bought their products, and went to their events. While doing so, I constantly thought about how I was different and how I wanted to be perceived. When I finally felt that I knew the industry well enough, I had tough choices to make— the same choices every up-and-coming expert must make: *How do I explain how I'm different? Why is my content valuable? How much do I charge? What "level" do I want to play at?*

In choosing the answers to those questions, I was essentially forming my positioning in the industry. If I couldn't answer intelligently and thoughtfully, then I'd be just like everyone else, and no one would take any notice of me (or buy my programs). So I spent a lot of time purposefully and strategically differentiating myself and my content. You should do the same.

Uniquely, I also chose a somewhat controversial path. Despite the fact I was just starting out in the industry, I decided to position myself toward the top of the industry by charging the same amount, if not more, than the biggest names in the personal development and business growth spaces. I did this for several reasons. In sharing these reasons, I risk sounding egotistical, but I hope that by now you realize I don't have a big ego. I just think sharing my thought process might help me make the point I want to make.

First, I chose to charge premium prices because I felt that my story and my strategies for success were unique and transformative. I saw the effect they had on others, and the results were dramatic.

Second, my content synthesized so much "best practice" that I knew it was comprehensive and cutting-edge. Importantly, I also knew that my content was structured in a very practical and actionable manner. The number one complaint I was hearing in the industry at the time was that most seminars in our industry were either too conceptual or too "rah-rah."

People wanted real-deal, tangible training, so I structured all my content to meet that demand. I had learned a lot about world-class training and adult learning programs while a consultant at Accenture, and I brought those lessons to my work in this "expert industry."

Third, I felt that my presence and presentation style was distinct and more engaging than others. Of course, this sounds odd to say, if not downright arrogant. But I personally found most experts and presenters to be tragically stoic, monotone, and rehearsed. The reality is that most people just do not push themselves to be good performers. This, I believed, was a great opportunity for my style—accessible, lively, enthusiastic, engaged and engaging, and authentic—to stand out. Years later, at Experts Academy, Paula Abdul would tell the audience she loved me because I was a "Chihuahua on crack."

Fourth, I chose to make my seminars more about training content than about hyping people up with affirmations only to pitch them a dozen new programs. This was a critical distinction in my career, perhaps the hallmark of my success. At the time, many seminars were simply one-day events that sold people into other high-priced programs. Or they were lineups of a few dozen speakers who all sold something from the stage. These "pitchfests" were all the rage because they are incredibly lucrative, and I participated in many. But I also saw that they had no future.

I made a financial decision to hold longer-format training seminars: three- and four-day events. I also decided to sell fewer programs from the stage, again favoring content and training.

Fifth, I came to find that my training materials and my approach to live events as well as to business were very different from the norm. Simply put, I was obsessive about quality and excellence, while many others, if not most, seemed to be missing the mark. As an example, most seminars in the industry were being held in cheap, dark hotels. The handouts and materials distributed to participants were on cheap paper and were basically photocopies of photocopies crammed into cheap binders. Worst of all, little attention was given to ambience and music. I decided to book nicer hotels and conference rooms that had windows. We lit our rooms more brightly, distributed high-quality handouts and binders, focused on better sound and lighting, and so on. I brought to my brand a higher level of corporate professionalism and dedication to detail, and it stood out right away both with customers and with peers in our community.

Finally, I decided to meet all the other leading experts in my industry. I approached them or their organizations and offered to add value, interview them, speak on their stages, quote them in my work, promote their products, or have them speak at my events. Soon I was friends with almost every other major expert in my industry. They then started promoting me to their audiences, which improved my positioning even more as wider audiences started seeing my affinity and affiliation with the "big names."

All this led me to believe that I was distinctive enough to charge premium prices. And it was these points of distinction and this level of pricing that quickly positioned me atop the expert community. Within a year of starting my seminars, we were selling out every event. This was during a time when the economy was failing and most experts were struggling to fill live events.

The takeaway here is that how distinct you are and how much you charge and stay connected with your peers is vitally important to your positioning in our community. You need to be incredibly conscious of these things because your goal is to quickly, strategically, and ethically elevate your presence in our expert community so that you stand out, attract more customers, and create a brand that your peers want to be a part of and promote.

I often tell my clients that to stand out they have to strategically and consistently position themselves in three ways. First, they have to position themselves as a credible source on their subject. How do you do that? You put out valuable content for free in the marketplace and online so that people can see who you are and how you are different. You create and distribute blog postings, videos, webinars, teleseminars, podcasts, eBooks, and so on. Obviously, you don't have to do each of these, but you need to get your message out there. And, yes, you need to put it out there for free so people can get a taste of who you are.

Second, I tell clients that they need to position their information as leading-edge training content. They need to be certain and direct in telling customers, "Hey, guys, here are the latest results and research I've been able to gather and get. This is cutting-edge stuff and I've structured it so you can quickly understand it and implement it." The more diligent you are at creating great training, the more people will see you as a high-value content provider. My personal dedication to this concept has helped my products and programs sell themselves and has caused people from all over the world to flock to our training. When people know that your content is the best out there, they trust you, believe in you, and, yes, buy from you.

Finally, I advise clients to get very close to the other experts in their field. Go to their seminars, mingle with them at conferences, join masterminds with them, promote them, and offer to add value to them and their business. As in any other industry, to some degree, you flourish based on who you know and whom you are associated with. So hang out with leading thinkers, interview them for your audience, and ask them to do the same for you with their audiences. Create great relationships. Get in the guru loop and stay there.

Positioning yourself and your content intelligently is both a skill and a mandate for succeeding in the industry. This work is all about creating distinction, value, and a good reputation in the industry. I focus on it with every communication I send out and with every program I develop. You should, too.

Expert Signposts:

1. The lessons I learned here about positioning are…

2. The steps I will take to position myself in this industry are…

3. The people I need to get close to in this industry are…

4. The way I want to be perceived in this industry is…

Messenger Mandate #2: Packaging

At the most basic level, messengers and experts are *content creators*. We find out what our customers want and what would improve their lives or grow their businesses, and then we go out and create some informational products and programs that serve them. We are creators.

And just like positioning, creating and sharing great information that is valuable to people is a skill and a mandate for experts. I like to use the term "packaging" to describe three activities that allow us to build a real business with a great reputation.

First, experts need to learn to *package their information* in a way that their customers can easily understand and implement. Despite the media's best attempts to force experts to hone their advice into three to five tips, the packaging of our advice is not that simple.

Outlining, chunking, ordering, and structuring our message are skills that take time to hone. The truth is that most people have no idea how to even think through the vast amount of knowledge they have about life or business. They don't even know how to communicate their advice so people can understand it well enough to actually use it. And they rarely know how to present it in a way that customers find engaging and empowering.

I teach a lot about content creation at Experts Academy, but let me share my favorite distinction in creating and structuring highly valuable content.

Have you ever wondered why a college professor gets paid less than a professional consultant? Or why a self-help guru gets paid more than a therapist or a counselor? Obviously, it has a lot to do with positioning in the marketplace. It also has a lot to do with how they package their information.

The college professor creates and shares information, just as all experts do. The realm of the professor generally lies in sharing *concepts* and *theory* about a given topic. The ordering of their information is geared to helping students gain a broad perspective on a given topic so that they can understand it and, hopefully, develop critical thinking skills. Forced by time and tradition, the professor flies high, giving a broad overview of the topic at the 30,000-foot level. Learning and thinking are the outcomes.

The professional consultant, though, approaches education in a very different manner. Consultants focus less on concept and theory and more on *process* and *practical methodology*. The ordering of their information is process and system driven, geared to helping learners move directly and efficiently, step by step, from point A to point B. The goal is not so much to help learners develop critical thinking skills as it is to build an actual ability or skill set to achieve a specific outcome. Freed from traditional educational constraints, the consultant puts the rubber to the road and addresses what learners actually do to implement concepts and theory "in the trenches and on the ground." Implementing processes and achieving results are the outcomes.

Now, before I start getting mail from academics around the world pointing out how wrong I am, let me qualify the example I've just given. First, it's a broad generalization meant to illustrate a point. In no way am I suggesting that professors are not as valuable, skilled, well intended, capable, or, for that matter, process-driven as consultants. For the record, I'm a tried-and-true supporter of traditional education. I'm a product of a liberal arts education, and I personally wish for every person to have an opportunity to get a college degree. College was in many ways the most developmentally rich and the most enjoyable time of my life. I believe that all my college professors and educators should be paid many times what they now earn.

But I hope you see the point in my comparison. Right or wrong, those who teach process and implementable solutions are more valued in the marketplace than those who teach concept and theory. Teaching step-by-step information is more valuable than teaching overview. If someone, especially a consumer who has never met you in person, is going to buy your informational product or program, they want to know that they will get advice and information that they can follow to get directly from point A to point B.

I cannot stress this enough. I've helped clients raise their prices by a factor of ten in dozens of subject areas simply by advising them to create a clearer and more implementable system, which their clients could follow to solve a problem and achieve a very specific outcome.

Thus, to package your information well, you must be clear about what your customer wants to overcome and achieve. Then you must create a step-by-step process that shows them how to achieve their goal. The better you do this, the more value you add. The more value you add, the more you can charge. The more value you add and the more you charge, the better positioned you are.

Second, experts need to learn to *package their products* well. If you are going to create a six-disk audio program with transcripts and an accompanying workbook, your program needs to be logically laid out and beautifully designed. This should go without saying, but because many up-and-coming experts are just starting out, they skimp and create everything on the cheap. Personally, I think 80 percent of the products in our industry look horrible. Just as Apple made a killing by reinventing the look and feel of personal computers and mobile devices, so, too, will experts who make their products beautiful and intuitive.

To you who are concerned with designing products yourself, take heart. It's very simple to work with a product designer and manufacturer in designing your product. The message here is not that you need to become a graphic designer or product designer; it's that as owner of your empire you need to make sure everything looks great.

Finally, experts need to learn to *package themselves* well. You have to present to the world a very organized, articulate, caring, credible, happy, and healthy person. It's a hard reality for many to swallow, but looks matter. If you are a sloppy, uninspiring mess, people won't want to follow you. If you can't take care of yourself or follow your own advice, why would anyone believe in or buy from you?

To anyone worried about appearance and beauty, don't—this is not an industry of Barbie and Ken dolls. You don't have to look like a magazine cover model or a movie star to get ahead. Lord knows my good looks are not the reason I've gotten where I am. I would argue that most experts in our community are actually, um, *plain,* your average next-door neighbor. The difference is that the highest-paid experts exude success because they identify themselves as successes, and they dress and carry themselves like successful professionals.

If you want to stand out in the industry, dress well, speak well, and carry yourself well. Project the strength and energy within you that cares and is enthusiastic about the world. Don't try to be something you are not, and please don't be another loud and overcompensating charismatic. Just be the best you, always, and especially when you are in the spotlight. In all your photos, websites, videos, products, and presentations, display the best of you. It's key to your brand and positioning. Never forget that you are a role model for others. Good health and buoyant energy are something we should all model to the world.

Expert Signposts:

1. The lessons I learned here about packaging are…

2. When creating my information and my products, I am going to package them so that they are…

3. The way I want my brand to be displayed to the world shows me as a person who is…

4. The actions I am going to take to keep fit, healthy, and energized include…

Messenger Mandate #3: Promoting

Once you create your positioning and packaging, it's time to alert the world to who you are, what you teach, and what you offer. It's time to promote yourself.

I'll bet this terrifies you. I always joke that if it were true that experts are ego driven, then they would not be so scared to death to be self-promotional. The reality is that most up-and-coming experts are terrified of the idea of "marketing." But the good news is that marketing in our industry is *very* different from what many expect.

First, let me dispel a common myth. Many trainers in our space often say, "Your number one job is to be marketing yourself all the time." While the intention is valid, the message is not. Your number one job in this business is to *teach and serve* people. That's what you felt compelled to do and that's what you must do. Luckily for you, we are at an interesting crossroad in time when *training is marketing.*

In the old world of marketing, experts would send out one-off promotions to their customers, announcing they had a new product available. For example, an author would send out postcards, brochures, and e-mails out of the blue announcing their new book. They would say, in effect, "Attention, I know I haven't talked to you for a while, but by golly, I have something that can help you. Buy my stuff now!"

This "announcement marketing" strategy never really worked well, and these days it's completely useless. The better approach for experts today is to add value to your consumers for free by actually teaching and training them on your topic. The idea, as I have referenced previously, is for you to send out a few free content pieces—free calls, videos, webinars, or eBooks, for instance—over a series of days or weeks. Then say, "Dear customer, if you like those things, then you will *love* my new program." The distinction is subtle but meaningful: Never sell without first adding significant value. It's the difference between promoting and campaigning. By giving away free content first, your customers get to reengage with who you are and what you have to offer them. Then, when you say that you have something for sale, they have a better understanding of the value, and a higher anticipation and likelihood of buying.

To promote your message, brand, and products effectively, what you need is a website and a shopping cart system that will allow you to capture a customer's contact information, send out e-mails, and process credit card orders. Most people in our industry start out with shopping cart services like 1shoppingcart, Office AutoPilot, or Infusionsoft. Once you have the online infrastructure up to add value, capture leads, and make sales, then the rest of your efforts revolve around relating to your customers and creating products and promotions. That, in a nutshell, is your new career.

The key to doing well with your promotions is to understand buying behavior and sales psychology. Most of Experts Academy has been built to teach this and give specific campaigns to authors, speakers, coaches, seminar leaders, and online marketers. The basic concepts of promoting anything for purchase, though, are universal. There are eight elements present in any good sales message, and all of them must be used in your sales videos or sales copy.

Claim.

Every strong sales message must begin with a claim, a bold promise about what your product or service can help others accomplish. It's important to know that people rarely read past a headline or watch more than the first few minutes of a video. Why? It's not because they have short attention spans, though you might think that. Instead, it's because they are not hooked and enticed to watch more. They aren't grabbed by the eyeballs by a powerful and relevant statement or promise that makes them pay attention and want to learn more. That's the job of your claim: to grab interest. Your customers should read or hear your claim and say to themselves, "I simply MUST find out more about this." To accomplish this, your claim should highlight the benefits, results, newness, distinction, or wow factor of what you are offering.

Challenge.

What are the problems your customers are facing in life? How much are those problems costing them? What is preventing them from moving ahead? What will happen if they don't resolve these problems? These are the questions that you must address to create rapport with your prospects. Show them that you understand their world and their problems. Draw attention to how "bad" it really is, and how bad it will continue getting if something doesn't change immediately. Selling is really the art and science of illuminating other people's problems and inspiring them to commit to your solution. As cold and horrible as that might sound, it's true: Great promotions always make you realize there's something missing in your life and that you can have and should have more. Your job as a marketer of your message is to show people the *need* for what you are selling, by shining the flashlight on their challenges and what is necessary to overcome those challenges. But you must never portray yourself as someone who has never had to face those challenges yourself, which is why we need the next element.

Commonality.

I often say, "If you haven't been through it, they won't listen to it." This is a simple statement that reminds us that people listen to experts who are like themselves. One of the most common mistakes new experts make in marketing their message is to sound too perfect and too successful to be believable. They forget what the great educator Booker T. Washington once said: "Success is to be measured not so much by the position that one has reached in life as by the obstacles which he has overcome." People relate to your struggles more often than to your successes. So never forget to share that the challenges your prospects are facing are *common* and that you have encountered similar obstacles on your path to success. Also, share how you and the prospect have a common and successful future. Say something like "I understand where you are. I've been there. We are in this together and I'm here to help you. We're going places, you and me." Your common story and journey to overcome challenges creates remarkably powerful rapport. Once you have rapport with your prospects, the next step is to show why *you* are the person to help them get ahead.

Credibility.

You create credibility by sharing the reasons why you are qualified to help your customers overcome their challenges and improve their life, results, or situation. For experts, this is accomplished by sharing the results you have attained in life, the research you've compiled and synthesized, or the reasons why you are a role model. This is not a time to brag about every little thing you've done in life, nor is it the place to brag about your résumé or riches. Instead, this is where you want to share your story of finding the solution that finally helped you achieve your breakthrough. This is where you say, in effect, "I have traveled the road you're on today. I've already reached the destination, and I'm here to shorten your learning curve and your path to success. I've done it and I've helped others do it, and here's *proof*." Next, you show proof that you are credible by highlighting your accomplishments as well as the achievements of others who have succeeded because of your advice or solution.

Choice.

No sales message can be effective if it fails to create a clear and powerful choice in the prospect's mind. You must present your product, program, or service in such a way that it is *obviously different and better* than anything else out there. Be bold in bemoaning why other offerings in the marketplace are insufficient or ineffective. State strongly and specifically why your solution is the best available to date. Show all the benefits that your solution will bring into your prospects' lives, so that they *want and need* it. Here's one secret out of the hundreds of marketing secrets we teach at Experts Academy: Show testimonials of customers stating explicitly *why they chose your solution*. This creates social proof and begins the argument in your prospect's mind to make a similar choice.

Comparison Pricing.

Everyone in the world wants a good deal. They want to know that when they buy something its value is much, much greater than what they paid for it. Knowing this, you must never present the price of your offering without first building toward a higher value. You want the prospect to think your offering is going to be more expensive than it turns out to be. You do this by price juxtaposition—showing big numbers and high value and then scaling down to a lower number but equally high value. For example, if you're trying to sell something at $19.95, you should illustrate how similar solutions cost hundreds of dollars, or how your solution can earn them hundreds if not thousands of dollars, and so on. If your prospects don't think your solution is going to be *ten times* the price you ultimately offer them, then you're not doing a good job. Again, you must do all this ethically and intelligently, but the takeaway should be clear: Make them feel that they are getting a great deal.

Concern.

What are the likely objections your prospects will have to buying your solution? What do they doubt about you? What do they fear won't happen when they get your product, program, or service? Answering these types of questions in your mind and in your sales message is *critical* to your success. The more objections you obliterate during your sales messaging, the more sales you make. Great marketers spend enormous amounts of time writing out the objections and frequently asked questions their prospects may have in their decision-making processes. You should, too. Personally, I never sell anything without first conducting informal tests with friends, strangers, and previous customers. I tell them what I have. I show them my products and sales videos, and then I ask, "What concerns or objections do you think someone might have to buying this? Would you personally buy this right now, paying cash, on the spot? Why or why not?" The lessons I learn from these tests translate directly and explicitly into my sales messages.

Close and call to action.

Making a strong close and call to action would seem like a no-brainer, but almost every new marketer I've ever met fails here. A great call to action builds to a crescendo, stacking on so many exciting benefits, bonuses, guarantees, and urgency messages that the consumer thinks, *I must* buy this *now!* Let's unpack that last sentence. A great call to action stacks messages. First, it stacks benefits and bonuses—*more* reasons and value for the prospect to buy right now. That's why in every infomercial you've ever seen offering some silly product they always double the offer at the end. *Yes, you get not just one, but TWO ninja Ginsu knife sets when you order right now!* Second, great closes remove risk and set the prospect at ease: *Hey, if you aren't fully satisfied with this product, then return it within 30 days and we'll refund your entire payment.* Guarantees are incredibly important in our industry. While most newbies fear that they will be taken advantage of for offering a guarantee, the fact is that more people will buy your offerings because of the guarantee than will abuse it. Next, a great close ends with scarcity or urgency messaging, telling the prospect why they must buy now or risk losing this great value, price, or one-time offer. Finally, a powerful close must end with a clear, direct, simple, and repeated call to action: *Click the button below right now to get started,* or *Call this telephone number right now to order.*

These eight components of a great sales message are simply an overview of good marketing. I hope they serve you in thinking about your next promotion. If you'd like to go deeper into the world of marketing your message, simply visit ExpertsAcademy.com and opt in by entering your contact information. I'm always sharing great marketing strategies and tactics with my subscribers.

Becoming a great marketer is like anything else—you master it by learning from others, doing it yourself, experimenting, testing, and improving. I encourage you to take marketing very seriously and to make it a lifelong study. Your message deserves to be heard by the masses, and you deserve to make money when serving others. To do so, you must become a great promoter.

Expert Signposts:

1. The next product or program I am going to create and promote is...

2. The benefits people would get from this program are...

3. The free pieces of content I can send to people before offering this program for sale are…

4. The reasons people will feel compelled to buy this program are…

Mandate #4: Partnering

In getting your message out to the world, you can go only so far by yourself. While everyone would love their message to go viral and suddenly make them an instant celebrity or YouTube phenomenon, it rarely happens, if ever.

This is an important point and something you need to know in advance. At Experts Academy, I've met hundreds of people who were just devastated that their message was not catching fire by itself. Many say, "Brendon, I just don't understand it. Everyone in the world *needs* my information. It's such an important message and can really change lives, but it's just not happening for me. What's *wrong* with people? They'll spread the message on YouTube about a puking cat but not my life-changing stuff! Help!"

This is funny on multiple levels. First, that's so true: Any animal that falls, pukes, bites, plays, or just looks cute will always virally trump your message online. Welcome to our society of insignificant distractions. Get over it and lose the ego. When the student is ready, the master will appear. Your message will grow virally as people need it and share it with others who need it.

It's also funny in a darker, more ironic way, because so many experts who love people and want to help people end up saying, "*What's wrong with people?*" Tragically, they become jaded, and without their being conscious of it, that feeling starts to creep into their communications as a subtle tone of condescension and exasperation. Then their message starts to die as people are put off. This is not funny—it's career ending. Never assume something is wrong with people simply because they don't like, believe in, or help promote your message. Everyone has their own agenda and needs, and when they need you, they will find you. Of course, that's assuming that you are "out there" to find via your website and promotions.

So what can you do to amplify your message and give it the best chances of going viral? First, create *great* value and content. Less obviously, go get partners who *make* it go viral. The goal of every messenger in the world should be to find more messengers to amplify their message. Even Christ needed disciples and promotional partners.

Landing big promotional partners is critical to your message's reach and your financial success. That's why it demands your attention and consistent effort. Luckily, it's a fairly straightforward process.

First, identify other experts on your topic. I've shared the importance of this previously. Your mission in your new career should include knowing *all* the big players on your topic in the industry. This would seem to be a no-brainer, but when I ask my audiences at Experts Academy if they can name at least ten gurus on their topic of choice, only 10 percent of the room raises their hands. The newbie's greatest disadvantage is ignorance, and nowhere is that ignorance more debilitating than on the subject of who else is out there teaching on your topic.

Scour the Internet for other experts by searching Google, YouTube, Facebook, LinkedIn, and all the usual search and social media portals. Who else is training people on your topic? Who has written a book on it? Who talks about it on their blogs? Who speaks about it for a living? Who is doing seminars? Who teaches it at major colleges and universities? While researching the Web for other luminaries and messengers might not sound like a lot of fun, it is necessary. It's also surprising to see what else is out there and what others are saying and doing. Luckily for you, most of what you will find is *crap,* and you will be inspired to take the helm and lead the industry on your topic.

As you're doing this homework, create a spreadsheet with all the other gurus' names, e-mail addresses, brick-and-mortar addresses, and websites. Don't worry, though. Finding their contact information is *easy*—there isn't a credible expert in the world who doesn't list their contact information on their website. Unlike celebrities, entrepreneurial experts *want* to be found, interviewed, and contacted for opportunities.

Also, subscribe to their newsletters as you go, so that you know what they send out to their communities. Their newsletters give you a great insider perspective on what they send out, sound like, and sell. I've personally

122 THE MILLIONAIRE MESSENGER

subscribed to over 100 lists, because I *want* to know what other experts are saying and doing, so that I am always in the know and relevant. I manage this by having a separate e-mail that I use to follow gurus.

After watching and following other gurus for a while, start weeding down the list to those you trust, like, and respect. That list becomes your target promotional partnership list.

Second, after you have done all this homework—and *only* after you have done the homework—it's time to reach out to these potential promotional partners. This is where 100 percent of newbies screw up. They reach out to other experts like idiots and amateurs. Their first communication usually says something like the following:

> Subject line: Please spread the word!
>
> Dear [insert name],
>
> I'm new to the industry and I like your work. I'm almost done reading your book. I'm also very passionate about [insert topic here] because [insert a very, very long-winded effort to explain life story complete with every major struggle recently that has forged character and summoned the message from soul]. With all that said, I have a new [insert thing here: blog, book, event, product] coming out in three days, and I would love it if you would [insert the usual newbie request to (a) give me something for free, (b) endorse my work, (c) send an e-mail to your entire list and tell them how great I am and to buy my stuff]. Thanks for doing that for me. Could you reply and let me know when you can do that? Attached is my [insert anything here: excerpt, article, résumé, other needless nonsense of massive megabytes that ensures delivery to spam box]. Thanks again for all you do. I really appreciate it.
>
> Signed,
>
> Naive Newbie

Clearly I am being facetious, but you get the point. Tragically, this really *is* what most people do when reaching out to influencers and leaders in their area. I know—I get around 100 e-mails *a week* like this.

Anyone who knows anything about Networking 101 can tell you why this is a horrible first approach. It's self-absorbed, needlessly long, and begging for a favor from a stranger. I have heard others in our expert community say these types of e-mails are equivalent to going on a date with someone, talking about yourself the whole night, and then trying to get a kiss at the end. But I disagree. It's more like walking up to someone and sticking your tongue down their throat. There's no date at all, just a pushy selfish act that gives the other no time to evaluate who you are.

The reason this kind of nonsense happens all the time is what I now call "secretitis." I'm guessing that if you are reading this book, you have heard about and probably read the book or seen the movie *The Secret*. It's actually a good book. The message is to send good intentions for what you want out into the world, and the universe will feel your energy and send you what you want. Before I criticize the book, I have to admit, I think it helped a lot of people. The book has a good message—your thoughts and what you focus on matter—and, in the interest of full disclosure, I'm friends with many of the stars in the movie. But even the stars later warned about the missing pieces of the message. The real secret to success involves a lot of hard work, but the book never mentions that. I believe *The Secret* is just another in a long line of self-help books that hypnotized our culture into leading their lives by a mantra of "ask and you shall receive."

If you have followed my work before, you've likely heard me tell audiences this, and you can quote me: The era of "ask and you shall receive" is dead; today's achievers live and breathe by the credo "*give* and you shall receive."

Before you can get you must give, and that's the first tenet of winning promotional partners to help spread your message and grow your business. The best approach in our community is to reach out to another expert and give them exactly that which you wish to receive. If you want them to promote your website, promote theirs. Want an endorsement? *Give* one first. Need their feedback on your project? Give them feedback on theirs.

With the "give and you shall receive" credo as foundation, here is an entirely different way to approach an expert who could be a potential promotional partner:

Subject line: Can I promote your work?

Dear [insert name],

I'm writing to thank you for all you do to help people, and to ask if I could promote your message and business to my circle of influence. I'm sure you are always looking for more people to help get your message out there. I know I am, so I'm writing to see if it would be okay if I zapped an e-mail to my friends, family, and fans about your work. Is there anything specific you are doing now that you are trying to promote?

I'm a big fan of your [insert relevant thing here: blog, book, product, event, etc.]. I particularly like your message about [insert their core message here], and it has meant a lot to me. I know it can be a thankless job being an expert, so please know that your work is making a difference in people's lives. It sure has in mine.

Anyway, since we're both in the business of [insert topic here], I thought I would share your message with my audience, even if my audience is not as large as yours. I help people [learn and achieve what?], so I think we have nice alignment in how we serve.

Thanks again for all you do. Please let me know what you would like me to tell my audience about and how I can help you.

Signed,

Nice Newbie

Nice Newbie's note is a complete 180 degrees from the Naive Newbie's note. It offers to add value. It gives. It's appreciative and to the point. It's open ended. It's good.

But hold on. You are an expert, which means that at some level you may often be overly analytical. This means you see a new opportunity or idea, and you immediately question it, instantly raising objections in your mind. Those objections often kill your ability to try new things and implement ideas. What am I talking about? Well, I know that as soon as you read Nice Newbie's e-mail you may have thought, *But wait a minute, Brendon! I don't have much of an audience! I don't have a big list of fans or subscribers! Oh, my God, this would never work for me! Why would anyone want to work with me?*

Am I right? I know this is true, because I've been working with experts for a long time.

Let's squelch your concerns by flipping this situation around. If someone wrote this e-mail to *you,* offering to promote your message, would you honestly care how many people they could reach? Sure, you would care, but would you say no? Of course not. You want to get your message out there to *anyone,* on any size list. This is akin to fund-raising in the nonprofit world. If a donor contacts a nonprofit and wants to give some money, the nonprofit doesn't mind if they get $5 or $50 or $5,000. Yes, of course, they would *prefer* $5,000 over $5, but they will take all the help they can get, and they are appreciative for all of it because they need help doing their good works. Well, so do you. A messenger rarely turns down help.

So after the expert writes back expressing appreciation and giving you something to promote, you promote it for them. You do this through your website or social media or whatever vehicle you have. You help them spread their message, no strings attached. Then you show them you followed through, by sending them whatever communication you sent out praising their work, and thus the relationship begins.

For those who object and say, "But, Brendon, what if they don't do anything for me after I promote them?" I respond, "So what?" You promoted some good content to your audience. If anything, your audience will appreciate the information.

But this is the more likely scenario: The guru is appreciative and asks more about what you do, and a real dialogue begins. Perhaps one day you meet live at a conference. At some point—and, sorry, there is no rule on when that point comes—you make a suggestion to cross-promote each other as "affiliates." What is an affiliate? It just means you promote for each other, track your results, and share in any revenue created by your promotion. It means you are promotional partners who make a profit together.

I could write an entire book about affiliate marketing, but instead let me give you the gist by offering another sample communication. When the appropriate time in the relationship comes, preferably after you have actually met your new guru friend in person, you say something like the following:

Subject line: Promoting you again

Hey, [insert name],

Got an idea for you. Remember when I promoted your stuff to my audience? They seemed to really like it. I bet we have a lot of overlap, and we could do a lot of good sharing of each other's ideas and products.

Here's my idea. I have a really high-value free [video, webinar, report, etc.] that you can give your audience. I've charged $xxx for this in the past, so they will really appreciate your hooking them up. I can send you a sample e-mail with a unique link to send out. When your people click the link they will go to a page where they have to enter their name and e-mail to access my free content and training. Once they opt in, they get immediate access. A few days later I will e-mail them and say, "Hey, if you liked that free thing I sent you, then you'd like my new [product or program]." Anyway, if they ultimately buy my new stuff—I'll know they came from you because it will track back to that unique link you sent out—then I'll give you half the revenue. So, you are giving superhigh-value free stuff to your list and making money for it. If you're game, I'll send you the custom e-mail and link to send your list. All you have to do is personalize it and click Send.

What do you think? This is important: I want to do this for you, too, so let me know what you'd like me to promote for you. I know now that my people like your stuff.

Signed,

Millionaire Messenger

This type of approach works great because it's based on open reciprocity (I promoted you; would you like to promote me?), value to customers (we'll give them free stuff), simplicity (just click Send), and compensation (you make money and so do I).

Nothing has to be complicated about all this, and you have probably seen it in action dozens of times. Here are a few good things to know about this approach. First, it works only if you have created a real relationship with your potential promotional partner. Second, it works only if you really add value to consumers with the free content. Third, you should disclose to your audience that you are an affiliate and may be compensated if they purchase anything through your links. Fourth, it's easy to set up using affiliate tracking and shopping cart functions from any basic provider like 1shoppingcart, Office Autopilot, or Infusionsoft. An important disclosure here is that I am *not* an affiliate or spokesperson for any of these companies, and I am not endorsing them here. I'm just sharing what most gurus use in the way of technology.

At Experts Academy, we often go into the intricacies and technology of doing all this, but the takeaway here should be obvious: Offer to make it easy and lucrative for someone to promote you.

Once you get a few promotional partners on board, it's like a multiplier for your business. More people in your space will find out about you, more people will subscribe to your list, and more people will start approaching you with their own promotional partnership ideas.

Promotional partnerships are not limited to other gurus, though. I've taught thousands of experts and entrepreneurs how to partner with Fortune 500 sponsors and nonprofit organizations through my famous Partnership Seminar. This event is the only comprehensive training seminar in the world teaching this. The basic idea is that you team up with companies or nonprofits to create unique content and promotions for their audiences, all based on your brand and how-to information. In exchange, companies and nonprofits often pay you, promote your message to millions, and provide invaluable perspective and resources (staffing, technology, etc.) to make it all happen. To learn more about organizational sponsorships and promotional partnerships, visit www.PartnershipSeminar.com.

Look, everyone needs promotional partners. If you agree with that, you should be diligently and strategically looking for potential partners who can help you spread your message and grow your brand and business. My promotional partners have helped me reach *millions* of people around the globe and make *millions* of dollars at the same time. They helped add value to people I could never have reached, and allowed me to become, in a wonderfully ethical and collaborative way, a Millionaire Messenger. I wish the same for you.

Expert Signposts:

1. The promotional partners I already know I want to approach are…

2. The value I could add to them is…

3. The next campaign I launch that I want them to support is…

4. The steps I'm going to take right now are…

The Last Mandate

Succeeding in the expert industry comes down to positioning yourself intelligently, packaging your information brilliantly, promoting your brand strategically, and partnering consistently to get your message out there in a bigger way.

The foundation for all these mandates—positioning, packaging, promoting, and partnership—is one enormously important though often uncelebrated mandate. I call it the Ultimate Messenger Mandate: Serving with Purpose. The truth is that anyone can go out there and lie about who they are and what they know. It wouldn't take a lot of effort to throw together some useful information and make yourself look good through marketing and phony third-party endorsements. Building an expert empire as a phony and a thief could be easy, and many have given our industry a black eye doing it. But there is just one problem: Acting in bad faith is not *good*—not for you or for our community. Most importantly, it isn't good for customers.

I wholeheartedly believe that the reason I've gotten so far so fast is because I believe in serving with purpose, and I consistently make it part of my message and my work. Others are smarter than I am, better marketers than I am, funnier than I am, and better looking and more articulate than I am. But I often outserve others because I *care* so passionately about my customers and their success. I never lose sight of why I am doing what I'm doing: to improve people's lives. I'm mentally, emotionally, spiritually, and financially driven by a higher purpose, and that makes all the difference in the world.

I say all this to illustrate that doing good and doing well financially can happen at the same time. The old idea that you have to choose between making a difference and making a fortune is dead in this new economy driven by both purpose and profit. We are in a wonderful new world of socially conscious consumers who care about who they buy from and how their lives are turning out. When you offer them value and you come from a place of service and purpose, they feel it, and your business grows. You make a difference, and you make a fortune. Message and meaning and money mix in a wonderful way.

Expert Signposts:

1. If I brought more purpose into my work, this would happen…

2. The people I have seen not serving their customers have been…

3. Those who are serving with purpose and doing a great job at it have taught me…

4. The way I will stay grounded and focused on service in this business is by…

Chapter Nine

THE MESSENGER MANIFESTO
(Or The Great Industry Reset)

The expert industry is undergoing a sea change. New technologies and marketing strategies are allowing both legends and up-and-coming gurus to amplify their message more quickly and broadly than any of us could ever have imagined.

Customers are demanding greater value, more free content, and higher levels of access to, and interaction with, experts through social media. The old ways of making money in the industry, from relying solely on book sales or holding "pitchathon" seminars, are either dead or dying. In a world of instant celebrity and worldwide broadcasting at the push of a button, there is more competition for eyeballs and business. Creating a fan base is at once easier because of social media and harder because everyone now has fans. The big names that led the expert community for decades are making way for a new generation of gurus.

All this has both positive and negative implications. But one thing is resoundingly positive: *Content is king, and the new kings of the economy will be the content creators.* The world is looking to us for new ideas and how-to information that can improve lives and grow businesses. It is an incredibly exciting, lucrative, and meaningful time to be an author, speaker, seminar leader, coach, consultant, and online marketer. I've felt this energy in a very palpable way at my live Experts Academy events.

But underneath all the opportunity and energy, there is also a great industry "reset" taking place. Part of this is because of technology, and part of it is because the old guard is quickly aging and retiring. The main reason for the great shift, though, is coming from the fact that a few leaders of the expert community are finally thinking of it as an *industry*. For the first time ever, people who give advice and how-to information out to the world and profit from it are actually thinking of what they do as a *career* in a *real industry*.

It seems lately that I'm taking both praise and jeers for leading this shift. Perhaps I deserve both. Some have said I'm doing a great job championing the charge; others have questioned my "right" to do so. Some have cheered my transparency about how the industry works; others say I talk too candidly about specific gurus' business practices. Some say I was too brash and audacious in creating the new Experts Industry Association; others say it's about time.

For the record, I believe they all are right. To give the backstory and share some perspective on the industry reset and my role in it, let's look specifically at six ways the industry is shifting and why. The first three changes have to do with how our community interacts internally. The last three ways have to do with how the industry faces outward to our customers.

An Internal Revolution

The shift inside our community has been, to many newbies, subtle. But the results are gathering like a tidal wave and are forever changing the nature of how we do business and help our customers. Three shifts are driving this change.

Reset #1: From Silos to Sharing

When I was a human performance and organizational development consultant at Accenture, the world's largest consulting company, I learned an invaluable lesson that's helping me and others both explain and lead the shift in the expert community. During my time there, I witnessed massive organizational change efforts at many of the top retailers in the world, including JCPenney, eBay, BestBuy, Nordstrom, Levi's, and Walgreens. Many of these change efforts either succeeded or failed based on how well teams within the organizations worked together and shared information and best practices from other businesses within the retail industry.

I've since come to believe that you can take any business or industry in the world that does not collaborate well or share best practices, and improve its earning potential by a factor of ten, in eighteen months or less, simply by helping it do so.

With this belief in place, to say my mind was blown when I entered the expert industry would be an understatement. To my complete shock, almost no one in the community was really sharing best practices in how they spread their message or built their business. The industry was disconnected, and almost no one knew what worked across businesses and consumer groups. It was mystifying to me, so I started asking many of the top experts in the world *why* this was the case. They were wonderfully frank and giving in my interviews. Three themes began to emerge that could explain why the industry had been so "in the dark" and disconnected from itself.

First, we have to understand that the expert community is made up of entrepreneurs who mostly work from home and alone. With no employees, no coworkers, no managers, and no regular contact with their peers, it's easy to see why they don't feel a part of a larger community. They are truly "solopreneurs."

As an employee in traditional organizational America, your peers are around you every day from eight to five. You see them at their desks, in meetings, at the water cooler, and at annual conferences. It's easy to consider yourself part of something larger, because you are around so many people. And when you're around people at work, you tend to share casually what's working and what's not.

But experts don't have that experience. They are often toiling alone creating their content, like artists. Though their lives may be seemingly public while they are sharing their information in books or onstage or on the Web, the opposite is true. Their lives are quite private, even isolated. In fact, the more popular they become, the more barriers are built around them to protect their privacy. Worse, without regular connection and communication with their peers, experts end up reinventing the wheel over and over. No one knows what works. No one knows what doesn't work. Everyone is adrift, trying to figure out how to get their message out there in a bigger way.

All this leads to an industry that does not "see" itself. Our members do not consider themselves connected or part of the same whole, despite the fact we all are essentially doing the same thing—marketing our advice, knowledge, and how-to information to consumers and organizations. That's why, as one of the first to publicly and consistently emphasize that we are a real industry, I've become a sort of ambassador for the expert community.

To be fair, there are organizations within the industry that have attempted to bring people together. The challenge is that these organizations also approached the industry as a set of silos. There are writing conferences and associations for writers, speakers' associations for speakers, coaching associations for coaches, and so on.

The challenge in chopping up the industry in this way is that experts rarely learn the multiple skill sets they need to earn multiple streams of income. If you are just an author and don't know anything about speaking, seminars, coaching, consulting, and online marketing, then you are boxing in your message—and leaving millions of dollars on the table. A speaker who doesn't understand online marketing is doomed to a life on the road, away from family. Coaches who do not know how to monetize their knowledge through books suffer, and so on.

That's why I decided to start Experts Academy in the first place. I wanted to share the industry's best practices across the silos for authors, speakers, seminar leaders, coaches, consultants, and online information marketers. I've done that successfully for years but decided to take it to the next level with the creation of the Experts Industry Association. Rather than just hosting a one-time seminar, I wanted to bring together the entire community on an annual basis. I also wanted to create something beyond me—Experts Academy is mine, but Experts Industry Association is *ours*. It's an organization that is not about me, though I'm one of its founders, but rather about all of us. We're going to get together each year, share our best practices, build bonds, set new standards, honor our heroes, and empower new generations to succeed.

I will likely get a lot of flak for having the audacity to start such an association, but I think it's time we all came together. Almost every industry in the world gathers to see how it can set new standards and grow as an industry. Why not us?

The second reason we've been such a disconnected and individualistic industry: Many experts fear one another. It's ironic that a community that prides itself on helping people overcome fear is so fearful of its own members. Experts are notoriously terrified that someone else will "steal their idea." In this way, I would argue that this is one of the most fearful industries in the world outside the inventor community—another group, by the way, that never grew up and considered itself an industry.

The misfortune of this reality is that so many experts hold their information and business practices so close to the chest that no one is learning from anyone else. Everyone is constantly reinventing the wheel or throwing stuff at the wall to see if it sticks. Aside from a few elite and often inaccessible and outrageously expensive mastermind groups, experts rarely share their best ideas about "the business" with one another. They are irrationally fearful that someone will rip off their training content or marketing strategy. While any businessperson can understand a desire to protect proprietary ideas, the level of fear in our community hurts us—it has hurt us for decades, and it will continue to do so unless we change our approach. If we don't start sharing what we know openly, how will we, as a collective group of experts, ever advance our industry?

My personal belief about sharing information stems from this metaphor: If you never let the baby out of your arms, it can never go out in the world and grow up. I believe that any idea I have can only get bigger and better if it is exposed to the world. While the amount of training I put out in the world is staggering, I've found that more people use it and buy it than blatantly steal it. Besides, with the ease of search and social media available to us these days, I would certainly find or hear about anyone illegally using my content. Here's the number one reason why I don't fear thieves and why I openly share everything anyway: I know I'm a creator. Even if someone were to steal all my training ideas and content today, I'm confident that I can create new information tomorrow. Experts are students and creators, and we can always create more useful information.

Let's go further. It is not just a worry that our content will be stolen. Everyone fears that their marketing strategy will be stolen. But who cares? Knockoffs and copies never do well, anyway. It's time we all admit that sharing our business models and marketing ideas will only help all of us do better in the marketplace. And the better we all do, the better our community will be perceived. I personally want others to model best practices so our reputation as an expert community grows. Makes sense, right?

Third, the industry is disconnected and still in its infancy because many of the old guard failed to look outside themselves to the future of the industry. This is my most controversial observation, and I know I will continue to be accused of many things for making this assertion. But the facts are the facts: Gurus have failed to groom new gurus.

This is evident in so many ways. Tens of thousands of people have failed trying to start in this industry, because there has been no collective wisdom shared openly about what it takes to succeed—there has been no roadmap. If you want to start a real estate business, there are *hundreds* of books on the shelf about how to do it. But how many books like this one have you seen? Why is this one of the only books to address the expert space as a real career and a real industry with best practices that anyone can follow to get ahead? Lack of general consumer information and training about our industry says a lot. And what it says is not positive.

There is no clearer evidence of the gurus-do-not-groom assertion than what I call "the open bench." In every Fortune 500 company in the world, there is always talk of a succession plan, a plan for new leaders to emerge when the current leaders leave their jobs or retire. There are plans in place to groom the next generation of leaders—talent and skill development plans, mentoring programs, and so on. Corporate managers and executives are always asked to share how they got where they are. The same thing happens in sports—you've got the A players out there, but on the bench the B players are being groomed and waiting to step up.

But where is the "bench" in the expert community? Think about it. Who in the personal development arena will be the next Tony Robbins? Who is the next Wayne Dyer? What happens when Oprah retires? Who is in line behind Deepak Chopra and Marianne Williamson in spirituality; David Bach, David Ramsey, Robert Kiyosaki, and Suze Orman in personal finance; John Gray and John Gottman in relationships; Gary Hamel and Clayton Christensen in innovation; Seth Godin and Jay Conrad Levinson in marketing; Rick Warren and Joel Osteen in religion; John Maxwell and Warren Bennis in leadership; Brian Tracy and Jeffrey Gitomer in sales; Andrew Weil and Mehmet Oz in health; and Dean Graziosi and Donald Trump in real estate? Of course, these are just a few of the top leaders in a few sample fields. I bet you couldn't name even a handful of people in each of these areas with major exposure, and I think it's time we start to ask *why not?*

This question led me to ask many of the people I just mentioned how they built their businesses, so that we could share that information with future experts. Indeed, many of the people I listed have spoken at Experts Academy, revealing exactly how they did it, including Tony Robbins, David Bach, and John Gray. What's fascinating in the case of Tony, David, and John is that each of them was actually shocked when I first asked them to reveal how they built their multimillion-dollar empires. They each had to create an entirely new presentation, one they had never before delivered even though they have all been training for two or more decades. It turns out that no one had ever asked them to speak specifically about how they built their expert businesses.

What was more extraordinary was that most gurus do not even think people are all that interested in learning how to step into their shoes. I personally don't think Tony ever fully knew until recently how many people wanted to have a career like his. The person introducing a session I was going to be conducting at Tony's famous "Unleash the Power Within" stage asked the audience something like this: "How many of you would love to have a career like Tony's and help people with your advice and motivation?" Almost every hand in the room went up. There were over 2,000 people there. To a degree, all those who follow us or learn from us see something of us within themselves.

Another issue is that many experts feel we are so unique that nobody can do what we do. This, of course, *is true.* Nobody on earth is like Tony Robbins. Or like you. Or like me. But remember, Tony started his business as a "young kid" who was washing his dishes in his bathtub because his tiny apartment didn't even have a working kitchen sink. He had no certification or formal education that allowed him to do what he does. As Tony likes to say, he had no formal education, but he has "a PhD in results."

Clearly, no one can be Tony Robbins. He is a legend and has his own orbit. I admire him deeply, count him as a friend and mentor, and think he is irreplaceable. He is the single most impressive and inspiring person I've met in my entire life. But what he has learned about business can be taught, duplicated, and improved on. Starting and sustaining a business is a replicable practice, and more newcomers could sustain their businesses if more legends shared their lessons learned. I honor Tony and all the legends who have shared their insights at Experts Academy. We need more people doing this all across the industry and through multiple vehicles so that we can build the bench.

I'm doing my part the best I can. I issue free videos all the time to my list subscribers; I point them to other experts doing great things; I host Experts Academy and Experts Industry Association. In addition, more than 100 mentees are in my Empire Group Mastermind and are receiving my coaching and training so that they can get their message out on a grander scale.

Other industries understand this concept. Everyone knows that no one can replace Warren Buffett, Steve Jobs, or Bill Gates. But all three are working hard to train the next generation to step into their huge shoes. We must do the same.

I think we can learn a lot from both the corporate space and the hip-hop community. Yes, hip-hop—that community does a great job of honoring its legends. When you hear Jay-Z speak about rap, it's like a history lesson. But as much as he and other leaders honor its pioneers, they also disdain knockoffs and constantly look for and celebrate new talent. It's actually quite remarkable. In one interview, Jay-Z was asked about the new crop of rappers, and he immediately named 10 or more up-and-coming rappers with ease. That would be unlikely in our industry.

I know this was a long, roundabout way of saying, "We need to get together, share what we have learned, and groom a new generation of leaders." But because of the attention that falls on me as founder of Experts Academy and the Expert Industry Association, I had to take the opportunity to share the history and rationale. I'll move more swiftly through the rest of the resets.

Reset #2: Renewed Focus on Innovation and Distinction

The expert world is full of copycats. They are about to get a rude awakening and quickly be swept aside by a new generation of content creators.

While the last three decades were very kind to our industry, a slew of would-be experts grew up trying to emulate the legends. This has led to a community that steals its own stories, quotes the same passages, fails to create new content, and rests on the laurels of legends. Few are reinventing the game. That has to change.

As an example of this problem, there is nothing sadder to me than speakers who still use the acronym F.E.A.R. This is a common acronym for discussing fear: False Evidence Appearing Real. It has been used for over thirty years, and you still hear it all the time. It's sad.

Another example: trainers who use the starfish story. It's a great story but badly overused. If you haven't heard it, in sum: Kid throws starfish back in the ocean. Old man says there are so many starfish on the beach, why bother? "It doesn't make a difference," he says. Kid throws another starfish back into the ocean and says, "Made a difference to that one." This story has been attributed to Loren Eiseley.

Another: the Cathedral story. Man asks laborers what they are doing, and one says, "I'm busting rocks, earning a living," while the other says, "We are building a cathedral."

Yech. This is not a judgment of these stories—they're great. Instead it's a blasting denunciation of the unimaginative copycats who lack the care of their craft and career to create and share new stories, metaphors, and examples. Our industry has gotten a bad rap for being repetitive, unimaginative, and "soft" simply because we're not innovating and creating enough new ideas. I believe I echo all the top leaders of our community when I say, collectively, "Shame on us!"

Beyond recycling old stories, many have also failed to create new value in quite some time. We must never become a "staple" industry like the T-shirt and socks industry. We want to be Apple, releasing new, relevant, and pioneering ideas and products that move our industry forward. While many reasonably argue that Apple releases too many new shiny things—I have no idea how many versions of the iPod I own—the point should not be lost. We cannot rest on products and programs that sold well five years ago.

I remember sitting in San Diego with a top female trainer after she had just returned from a seminar that she had first attended 20 years earlier.

Her disgust inspired me to write this particular reset. She said, "Brendon, that seminar hasn't changed in twenty years! The person conducting that event hasn't grown or learned anything new in two decades? Worse," she continued, "is that no one has pushed [that guru] to change, because they follow like lemmings and are scared to say '*Evolve!*'"

Very, very few products or programs can stand the test of time. And even if they could, the creator of such a program owes it to his or her audience to deliver new value and information. It would be a disservice to put out a blockbuster program and then stop. Customers want and deserve mastery, and that doesn't come with just one program.

I get a lot of criticism for these arguments. Many people object to this idea by pointing out that many books, for example, are timeless, like those in the self-help genre. Personal growth concepts are always relevant in some way, they say. I agree. Books like *Think and Grow Rich, How to Win Friends and Influence People, The Alchemist,* and thousands more are awesome and will always be awesome (although many of even those books have been revised).

But my point is not that we should toss out the old. Rather, we simply don't have to keep rehashing old material. We have to challenge ourselves to continue delivering new ideas, distinct stories and perspectives, and cutting-edge information in new products and programs on a continual basis.

This can be difficult work, I know, and sometimes new ground is hard to find. It is also very common for new experts to cover old ground without knowing it. As they say, there is nothing new under the sun, and nothing new has been said since Adam. We all have to be comfortable with the fact that so much has already been said in this industry, what we are teaching may have been taught in some way before. If you ever get called out on this, either apologize for it ("Wow, thank you, I didn't know someone else had said that before.") or address it and explain your points of distinction ("Yes, I've heard someone has taught this before; here is how I'm different.").

This reality hit very close to home when I began. As you will recall, my car accident had inspired me to think about my life and ask, "Did I live fully? Did I love openly? Did I matter?" I had been sharing those questions rather broadly, probably for about three or four years. Then one day after a speech, a mentor told me that Norman Cousins had asked very similar questions decades before me. Cousins—whose work I have since come to admire tremendously but at that point had never heard of—found that people do indeed ask such things when evaluating their lives. Cousins wrote,

"The great tragedy is not death, it's what we allow to die inside of us while we live. When you are on your deathbed, you're not thinking about how much money you have or how much you have accomplished. The questions people generally ask on their deathbeds are: 1. Have I lived wisely? 2. Have I loved well? 3. Have I served greatly?"

You might think I was horrified to discover these similarities. Instead, reading Cousins' passage became one of the most validating moments of my life. I was so happy to find out that I was not the only one to believe these things. It made me feel connected to our universal values and experiences as a human being. It proved to me that what I knew to be true was true for others.

That said, I had to quickly begin explaining my perspective in my work to avoid any future issues. I recently found a speech transcript in my personal archives that showed me addressing this way back in 1999, long before I would become known for my three questions with the launch of my book *Life's Golden Ticket* in 2007. While it is a rather long passage, I thought including it here might help to show how you can openly and honestly address any similarities your life's message might have with others' work. The truth is that we all have common human experiences, and when sharing our life's message we will often overlap. But even if it has all been said, what *is* new is our own unique experience of learning our own lessons, getting our own results, and creating new value for people. I hope this transcript reminds you of that.

From the archives:

As I've been sharing since my car accident, which was the most important and yet terrifying moment in my life, I discovered a lot about myself and the world back then. When I was recovering I kept thinking about all that had happened. I still to this day remember those last moments of the turn, life about to disappear, and learning how important life was. I came to realize we'll ask if we lived fully, loved openly, and made a difference, because in that experience I wondered whether I was adventurous enough or really connected enough or had lived for something or someone outside of me. The sad truth is, I hated the answers. I was just a young, directionless kid who didn't know any better until I crashed into life's greatest lessons.

Since then I've volunteered at hospices, and I've seen so many people struggle with the same questions at the end: "Did I live fully? Did I love openly? Did I matter?" I think it's good to know those are the questions we may seek to answer at the end, because then we can live our lives so we'll be happy with the answers.

These questions are not just my unique findings. Last year a friend of mine showed me a passage from Norman Cousins, and it meant so much to me. It was validating and amazing all at once. It turns out Cousins had written long before me that people on their deathbeds ask, "Have I lived wisely? Have I loved well? Have I served greatly?" It was just so amazing that I crashed into a lesson that others had found to be true. In fact, if you know any hospice worker or end-of-life counselor, they will all say pretty much the same thing": "Yep, people reflect on their life, and they wonder if they really lived, and they wonder who they loved, and they wonder what impact they had." It's a universal thing, so I'm not seeking credit for it in any way—certainly generations of people discovered this before Cousins or I or anyone else ever wrote about it. I just hope to share my unique story and perspective.

The only thing that may be unique about my three questions comes down to word choice, I suppose. Cousins asked if we lived "wisely," but I wondered a different question: if we lived "*fully*." It's subtle yet important to me, at least in how *I* live. I want to live vibrantly and burst across the planet like a firework and make foolhardy decisions and have adventure. But who am I? Just some young punk kid, because Cousins said "living wisely" and Buddha used the same phrase when he said, "Even death is not to be feared by one who has lived wisely." Cousins also talked about "loving well," but I was probably too damn young to know what that meant when I forged my three questions. To me loving "openly" was my word choice because I had been so closed off from love as a young man after the breakup with the first woman I ever loved. It seems to me that whenever love goes wrong, it has a lot to do with how open we really were.

Anyway, the last word choice was important for me at the time, I guess, and says a lot about what I try to do now. Cousins talked about whether or not we "served greatly," which I think is such a great phrase. I guess when I crashed into reality I ended up thinking about it differently as a young man. I didn't think about serving greatly, though, as I said, I like that, because I didn't ever think I could make a "great" difference. I think many people don't think they can change millions of lives or do "great" and grand things that change the world. Some just want to make a difference with one person, and perhaps they don't consider that a grand or great thing, which is too bad. "We don't have to change the world; we just have to change *somebody's* world," is something I heard once. So I simply ask, *Did I matter? Not Did I do something great?* Maybe it's just a small thing. Did I matter? That's what I ask.

Of course, this is all just silly semantics, but it really meant a lot to me when I found that my accident and my experiences in hospices led me to similar conclusions that others had drawn. It helped me realize we are all on the same journey of life, discovering similar things. I hope we all try to share those similar findings even if they are worded a little differently or even if it's from our own perspective. It turns out, living and loving and doing good are universal values we all find important, and I hope sharing a little with you today about those values helped.

The takeaway of this section is this: Be distinct. Share your own stories and create your own content. Continually create new value that wows people. That's what will elevate our reputations and our revenues in this industry. If, for any reason, your work ends up being similar to others'— which, of course, will happen—address it. But do understand that *teaching points* can be similar in nature because of our universal human emotions and experiences, but our *training products and programs* should be unique to our brands. Does that make sense?

Reset #3: Better Branding

Ever go to a seminar and get a crappy binder full of "resources" that seemed to be photocopies of photocopies of photocopies? Ever receive in the mail a chintzy self-published book that looked as if it were designed by a gorilla? Or ever go to a guru's website only to see a postcardlike site that seemed from circa 1995?

I've asked these questions of audiences from around the world, and they all laugh and raise their hands in acknowledgment. It is funny but also tragic.

It's vital that as a community, we start making our websites, products, and programs *look better.* Just as Apple did to the personal computer and the mobile device, we must upgrade our industry's overall aesthetic and design. We need to be cognizant of the massive shift our society has experienced from function to form, from buying bland to buying creative, customized, and colorful. The world does not like crap or clutter, and we, as a group of professionals, are often guilty of creating websites full of both.

To put it bluntly, *our industry needs a facelift*. As an observer, I see three key areas that require a makeover, pronto. First, we have to refresh our websites to be more contemporary and interactive, which now means video-driven blogs with comment sections. We also need to make our membership sites look as if they are worth people's time and money. People should *enjoy* and *be proud* of being part of our online communities. When is the last time you had someone mention feeling that way?

Second, we *must* start making our shipped products look "retail ready." The DVD home-study programs, audio programs, binders, worksheets, and resources mailed out in this industry are abysmal. This is almost entirely across the board except for the top 2 percent. Believe me, I'm not a design snob, and I'm not into spending too much money on graphic designers. I understand there is still a core group of marketers teaching people to "get it done fast, get it done cheap, get it out the door now." I also know that many customers don't care what our information looks like—they just want the content and knowledge and don't care about the vessel.

All the objections to making our products look better actually make sense in a silo world. If we can stretch our field of influence to understand that we are a community with real careers in a real industry, we can understand that our community has a singular reputation. Unfortunately, crappy-looking products are like a ripple in the pond and affect the entire aesthetic of who we are. If we all step up and make our products look good, we can all enjoy the benefits of a more appreciative, impressed, and happier customer base.

Finally, we desperately need a makeover of our approach to doing seminars. With the exception of perhaps five to ten brands, the industry is still hosting seminars, workshops, and conferences in cheaper airport hotels with dim lighting, poor ventilation, and uncomfortable chairs. Worse, promoters are barely spending any money on lighting, sound, branding, and materials. It's a disgrace, and it would never happen in the best of the corporate world. Believe me, I know that it can hurt to spend a little more on these things—I do over a dozen live events a year and now spend millions making them run well. And I understand that customers want promoters to get low room rates for them at travel-friendly and accessible hotels. But it doesn't cost a lot more to find a great hotel, put up a few well-designed banners, hire some good AV people, and deliver nicely printed and bound seminar materials. This is perhaps more detail than people would imagine I should go into in a book like this, but we all have to relearn the phrase "details matter." Whether you are holding a free seminar or a high-fee seminar, your job is to make the learning environment look and feel terrific. We owe it to ourselves, and we owe it to our customers.

These three resets are powerful. When we move from an industry stuck in its own silos to a best-practicesharing and bench-building community, we all win. When we deliver creative, innovative, and distinct content and programs, we all elevate our game. And when we refresh our look and branding to be more clean and contemporary, we repair the cheap reputation we have been pinned with.

We can do better. It's our time to look at ourselves as a singular industry with a singular reputation that we can all affect and improve. The change must start within. The revolution and reset is already at hand. Join us.

The Outward Reset

The previous three resets focused on what we must do internally to improve our industry and reputation. The next three are actions we can take with our customers to continue the momentum.

Reset #4: Transition from Sales Communication to Value Communication

A curious thing happened in list management over the past five years. Gurus began mailing coupons to their lists, following corporate America's ineffective and poor choice at electronic marketing and communication. They also made a decision along the way that they would send *either* content-only newsletters *or* sales messages. This was just bizarre.

As I write this page, we are now caught in a moment when many experts are sending out too many sales-only e-mails. They do not send e-mails with value anymore, just links to sales pages or sales funnels. This must change and it must change now.

The reset in the industry will finally achieve balance between sales and value by combining them instead of forcing an either/or decision. If you are one of my subscribers, you know that almost *every* e-mail I send out adds major value, even if I'm promoting someone else's product or offering a sale of my own.

For example, I recently promoted a friend's informational course on social media. Almost everyone promoting the same course simply sent an e-mail to their subscribers that said, in effect, "Here is an awesome new course. Click here to buy it." There was no value offered, and thus their e-mails were what I call "sales-only communication."

I designed a different approach. I sat and thought about my customer and what I was doing in social media that was working well. Then I went into my video studio and shot an informational video explaining my best social media strategy. At the end of the video, I essentially said the following:

"I hope that serves you in your own business. If you would like more training on social media, I'm not really the expert, but you can click the link below this video to learn about my friend's new training on social media. I think you'll enjoy it a lot. If you happen to enroll in his course, I'll give you two of my training courses as congratulations. My two courses really complement his, so you'll be getting twice the value."

See? I added value by doing what experts do: *teaching*. I taught my subscribers something useful, and whether or not they bought my friend's program, they still learned something. So no one was upset, and no one was put off. Does this take a little more effort? Of course it does. But it keeps me in good standing with my list because it does what I promised them, which is to add value to their lives. The result was that I was the number one promoter of that course and made over $200,000 in affiliate commissions. Affiliate commissions mean that I was paid a percentage of the sale when people signed up for my friend's course, which I disclosed clearly to people in my video and on the page where my video was hosted.

This example illustrates that we do not have to choose between adding value and selling, and I think it's important that the community start doing this. Most of the successful gurus out there, including those in the online marketing world, are already leading the way and have been for a while. Now everyone else should follow.

In the sales arena, I also think it would be helpful if our community became more thoughtful in strategically planning our communications and promotional calendars. It turns out most experts don't actually *have* a promotional calendar planned out. Instead, they end up at the end of the month realizing, "Oh, I guess I'd better send a monthly newsletter today. I'd better figure out a topic to write about or find something to sell." This is just bad business and bad practice.

I've been very blessed to consult with many of the world's best retailers and have some perspective in this area. I remember speaking with brand managers at Nordstrom and BestBuy and being blown away by how far in advance they plan their promotional calendar and product releases. Retailers know what they are doing not just the next couple of months but in the next couple of *seasons* and *quarters*. We need to learn that skill and be more diligent about planning how and when we will add value and make sales.

Finally, as a last point on sales, I believe our entire community would breathe a sigh of relief if we all notified each other sooner about our upcoming promotions. I cannot tell you how many e-mails I get that say, "Tomorrow we are launching our new X; please promote for me!" Let's all give each other several *months* of notice on what we're doing, and forever put to sleep the last-minute monster.

With sales out of the way, let's talk about *value*. What constitutes value in the how-to world has evolved over the decades. No longer is a newsletter article sufficient to keep an audience engaged and served. Most customers tell me that value to them means they receive actual *content* and *implementable ideas* that they can act on right away. Sending people funny videos or short overview articles or blog posts is not value; it's distraction.

To serve your customers best, think about what their goals are, and send out useful training that helps them move from point A to point B. Give a simple-to-implement idea, but also give the bigger picture and process. Ask yourself, "If I received this communication, would I find it valuable personally and professionally, and would I be able to do something new and important after seeing it?"

Again, I understand that all this takes work. But it's what we were born to do anyway—to teach—and it serves the customer.

Reset #5: Achieving Customer Service Excellence.

Everything I've mentioned so far will do little to improve our industry's reputation if, at the same time, we don't improve our customer-service approach across the board. Bad customer service has become the expectation of customers, and because of this, fewer customers buy, and frankly, many have started to send jaded, aggressive, and flippant messages to get what they want. A friend of mine recently said, "Too many of the new customers in our industry act like skeptical jerks, and it's our own fault."

Since day one, I've been extremely, if not obsessively, focused on customer service. We have always made sure to respond to people at least on the same business day we receive a call or e-mail from a customer. We often reply within the hour, except during heavy promotional periods when we may be briefly overwhelmed. We make our trial, return, and refund policies clear in our videos, on our checkout pages, and in our terms and conditions for every product or program we release. To be fully transparent, I did get this wrong during one promotion when we were not clear enough about the refund policy, and it created unneeded angst and hassles later on. You often learn customer service the hard way in this industry. But in general, I would say we have a very strong and positive reputation for great customer service.

Unfortunately, that means very little these days. Yes, you heard me say it: Having a great customer-service reputation does not mean as much as you might think it would in this industry. Now, before I get critical e-mails for saying a good reputation is not important, let me explain *why* I say that. Two realities about the greater context of doing business as an expert will serve you here.

First, *most* of your sales on any given promotion these days come from buyers who have never heard of you, especially when you start out. I'm fairly well known, but a full 72 percent of the buyers of my last promotion had never heard of me. People who come into your sales funnel are often brand new prospects who have never heard of you and know nothing about your reputation. Because the expert community is not active on Yelp or other customer-evaluationoriented websites (yes, this will change too), there is really not much information out there about the personalities, brands, and companies in our industry. It's odd, because other industries are driven by community product reviews.

Second, because most people who buy from you have never heard of you, *they default to their preconditioned assumptions about the industry as a whole.* This is a *horrible thing.* I say this because historically, "gurus" have been so ego driven or adored by forgiving fans that they simply never focused on customer service as a business practice. It turns out that rock stars and celebrities, too, have abysmal customer service for the same reasons.

Because of this tragic track record with customer service, we all lose. Personally, I'm tired of getting customers who call or e-mail us in advance of buying and are jaded, rude, skeptical, or needlessly challenging with their questions. This is crazy because we probably have one of the best reputations in the expert community. We deliver what we promise, and more. We are responsive. We care deeply about our clients' success, and if anything, we overcommunicate our terms and conditions. Still, here's an unedited e-mail we received during my last promotion:

"Hey, I think I like your stuff and I think I'm going to buy it but I need more convincing you guys aren't like the other guys in this industry who rip us off and lie about refunds and guarantees. If I don't like your [insert expletive] stuff I want to know if I can return it right the [expletive] away otherwise I'm not going to buy it. So, let me know, are you guys honorable or thieves like everyone else?"

Doesn't that speak volumes about the preconditioned assumptions this person has about the expert community? You have to understand that *most* people approach the guru industry with this level of energy and caution these days. "Gurus" and experts in all industries have gotten a bad reputation in the past few years, and it's tragic. That's not the fault of anyone else but those in the community who spoil it for the rest of us.

With that said, I want to emphasize that I don't think most experts out there are bad businesspeople or acting without integrity or with any malice toward their customers. I strongly believe that almost to a person, our community is made up of deeply caring and committed experts. It's just that the bad few do taint the picture of all of us. And while almost everyone in this community is good and caring, they are, in fact, extremely busy and creative people who are running small businesses from home. *This leads me to conclude that it is distraction and lack of resources that have led to our industry's bad customer-service reputation.*

The good news is that this can all be easily and swiftly corrected if we all decide to flip the switch and reset our compass to focus on our customers as much *after* the sale as before the sale. At a financial level, we should all remind ourselves that the lifetime value of a customer is worth ensuring that they are happy, cared for, and well served.

Besides my doing my small part in this reset of practicing what we preach, we have also committed our team to ensure that the Expert Industry Association recognizes and celebrates brands known for excellent customer service.

Reset #6: Honor More, Expect More

In the late 1980s, there was a subtle but distinct shift in the tone coming from the expert industry. And it was not a good one. Gobbled up by the "greed is good" *Wall Street* mantra and the time period's celebrations of shock jocks and heroic CEOs, we went astray. Many self-help gurus and experts in every field started two poor practices.

First—and this upsets me greatly—experts started speaking and writing in a tone that smacked of condescension to their clients. Gone were the honoring tones of experts and writers of the past. Replacing them was the "bootcamp guru," the harsh-talking in-your-face expert who was clearly much more attuned to your problems and reality than you were. In fact, to these types of gurus, I say your whole life is out of whack. You are sleepwalking through your life. You do not know how bad your unconscious is derailing everything you do. You are screwing up your relationships and your job, and you are tossing aside your future. Oh, and you are lazy and foolish. And because of it, no one loves you. There! Did I forget anything?

While this may sound exaggerated, the most extraordinary reality is that people were basically saying this garbage. It still happens today! Pick up a self-help book, and it seems as if it were written for complete losers who have lost all control of their life. Authors in that space started writing and speaking to the lowest common denominator. It's as if the whole industry started sounding like that horribly screeching condescending phrase Dr. Phil became famous for: "*What were you thinking*, [insert "dummy" here and you've got the sound]?"

For the record, I like Dr. Phil's work, his books especially, and I think he's helped millions of people. I also think it's obvious that he uses that phrase with a sense of tease and humor that makes it palatable (sometimes), and that he truly and genuinely cares for his clients and audience.

But you get the point. Experts became very condescending and started writing and training as if they were advising either children or the most severely out-of-touch or maladjusted among us.

It's time for a new tone. It's time for us to honor our audience more. Let's assume that people are doing their best, not their worst, that they are capable, not inept, and that they are pretty tuned in since they did reach out to us for advice in the first place. Personally, I don't think people are out of touch or sleepwalking through their lives. Like most of us, people are very aware of their problems and their reality, and they are just looking for some inspiration and instruction to reach the next level. I have great respect and admiration for my clients and audience, and I speak to them as peers, not as their "guru," camp counselor, or drill sergeant.

Of course, at this point, it's common for people to say, "Yeah, Brendon, that all sounds good, but c'mon, man, you and I both know that the media reward shock and awe and the drill sergeant over the quiet servant." I sadly agree. But I also think we get to choose what kind of games we will play in life in order to be rewarded and recognized. Personally, I don't think it's worth my being someone else or bullying someone else just to get their attention or the media's attention.

Let's start believing in our customers and looking at them with as much admiration as they do us. By honoring our audience once again, we will bring a reputation of honor back to our industry.

Next, as much as we honor them, let's also begin expecting *more* out of our fans, followers, and customers. This chapter has been about us expecting more out of ourselves as leading experts, but now I want the emphasis to be about expecting more out of our *audience*.

I haven't been able to place my finger on exactly when it started happening (though my research and interviews point to the mid-1990s)), but there was a shift in the industry when suddenly it became *okay* and *casually well known* that our clients were not implementing what we were teaching them. Suddenly there was a laissez-faire attitude about the results our clients get when implementing our advice, ideas, strategies, processes, systems, and so on. "Well, I can't control whether they implement my training, so oh, well," went the attitude.

That attitude is so pervasive today that it has created an entire generation of experts who do little to set expectations, challenges, accountability systems, or follow-up programs with their customers. In turn, our industry's clients are not implementing and getting results, which in turn hurts our reputation yet again. It's time for a reset here as well.

I don't pretend to have all the answers, and like everyone else, I want more of my clients to actually *use* and implement my programs. Like everyone, I'd be happy if more of our customers would even *open* the book or DVDs they ordered!

In all seriousness, we can all start the reset immediately by changing our tone and verbiage with our clients. We can begin telling them directly that we only want serious students and that we *expect* them to take action. Sometimes just having someone tell us that we can raise our standards can be an impetus to actually change. We can instill the desire and challenge with them without being drill sergeants. All we have to do is be greater inspirations and enable our customers with more tools, goals, and follow-up communications. We can say things like the following and do it not for marketing but because it's true:

"Look, if you are like many of us, there are too few people in your life who are holding you to an elevated standard of excellence. People want to protect you and keep you safe, and they make it okay not to push yourself further and harder. But our paths have intersected because you believe you are capable of more, much more, and you are looking for new ways to reach your highest potential in this area. So let's make a deal. If you are a person who genuinely wants to succeed at this, and you are truly willing to implement what I teach, then let's begin. But our industry is full enough of tire kickers and fly-by-night gurus who just sell and run. So let's make a deal. You implement this stuff, and I will follow up with you with a reminder series from our system. We need more doers, and if that is you, then let's begin. But if you feel like just 'trying' my stuff out and dabbling in this area, then perhaps you should browse my blog but not become a student. I'm setting a high standard for my students, and I expect you to have a high standard if you become one."

Perhaps that's too hokey and not the best argument or marketing strategy. It's easier to say, "Hey, just buy my stuff, and we'll see if it fits you." But it's important that our programs inspire people to set a high standard and implement our ideas. Change often happens when we communicate differently to the marketplace, so this is an easy area to make a change.

Personally, I do my best to give my clients a very hard time if they don't do what they said they would. I hold high expectations for them and for myself. I try to give my customers the checklists, samples, and resources needed to take action. I can do better at this, though; I think we all can. Today is the day we must all begin.

A Tribute

I am keenly aware that in writing a chapter like this I run the risk of sounding negative and overly judgmental about our expert community. I will likely be harpooned on a few blogs for being too audacious or bigheaded in making these assertions. My goal here, though, was not to be negative or come across as flippant. I know I am but a bit player on the historical stage of this industry, and I didn't write this chapter for self-aggrandizement or to point fingers. My goal was to take full advantage of this platform to help you lead this industry. And to lead, we must all be transparent about where we are and how we can improve. Until we point out what is not working, we cannot fully serve our customers or advance our careers or community.

With that said, there's a lot that is *right* in this industry. Our work changes people's lives for the better, and that is extraordinary. Our community is the most creative, brilliant, thoughtful, and caring of any I have witnessed. I would happily challenge anyone to find another industry that has helped as many people live fuller, richer, happier, and more meaningful lives than ours has.

I hope you've sensed my joy, appreciation, and excitement for having the opportunity to have a career as an expert. This industry radically changed my life and has changed millions of lives before me. Now it's time to continue the good work of those who came before us and, at the same time, elevate our industry to the next level. I hope you will join us.

Chapter Ten

TRUSTING YOUR VOICE

We've come a long way. If I've successfully fulfilled the expert mission, then I hope you've felt inspired and instructed on how you can improve your life. You can make a difference and an income with what you know. Your advice and your life experiences are more valuable than you ever imagined. You can have a real career as an entrepreneurial expert if you simply position, package, promote, and partner with others to get your message out there.

You can do this. Now is your time. When you begin reaching millions of people and making millions of dollars, then you will have become a true Millionaire Messenger. Even if you never reach that level, sharing your message with any size audience will always be a meaningful act and a true path to purpose and fulfillment in life. There is meaning in mentoring other, and satisfaction in serving.

If you've read this far, then you now know more about this career and industry than I did when I began. I have earned millions of dollars with these concepts and helped millions of people. I'm excited to hear what you do with it all. You have a great foundation, and you have a huge head start on the next generation of gurus. In fact, you probably know more now than most experts who are practicing today, because until now few people have shared their best practices. If you run into up-and-coming or struggling experts on your exciting new journey, please give them this book or lend a helping hand. We all need to help and honor our fellow messengers.

I don't know why you are reading my words at this moment, but I feel honored that our paths have crossed and that I've been able to share with you what I've learned. I'm still learning. Experts are always students first. Still, it's been a great joy writing this book for you and our community.

After working with tens of thousands of experts and advice gurus worldwide, I do have one strong assumption about why you have landed on this page and found my message at this point in your life. I believe you are here because deep within you, there has been a restless stirring to share your voice with the world in a bigger way. Perhaps you picked up this book because you decided to share your life story and experience with others for the very first time. Or perhaps you have already been sharing your message and you were looking for new ideas and strategies for amplifying it more loudly, broadly, and profitably.

Regardless, I believe that your being here has something profound to do with your voice in this world. If that is true, I'd like to share one more story before saying good-bye.

About Sarah

Sarah was my student but ended up my teacher. When I was in graduate school, I had the opportunity to teach a few classes in public speaking. I was bubbling over with excitement about being in a position to lift up and educate students. I put my full effort into all my classes, reinventing ways public speaking had been taught and teaching with every ounce of passion I had. I was new to teaching, and in hindsight, I had no idea what I was doing. Still, I gave my all at the time, and I felt it was a deeply meaningful experience.

But as often happens with new teachers, toward the end of my first year I became worn out. I had taken on a lot that semester, and suddenly I didn't feel that I was making a difference anymore. And then I met a shy, reserved, withdrawn student named Sarah.

At the beginning of the semester, Sarah didn't seem like a troubled student. She was at every class and on time. But soon she was in trouble. She skipped her first two speeches—she just didn't show up on her assigned days. This alone guaranteed her failure in the course. And yet, even after missing those two crucial days, she showed up on time every day for class. I kept trying to chat with her after class, but so many other students would be asking questions that Sarah always seemed to slip quietly out of the classroom before I could speak to her.

Three weeks before finals, I posted the speaking assignments for the class, listing who would speak on which day. Sarah's name was not on the list. She had never given a speech and had already failed the class, so I didn't include her. A few days later, as I was helping another student during my office hours, I saw Sarah enter the office, looking rather sheepish. She chewed her nails and kicked her feet the entire time she waited for me to finish with the other student.

When at last we spoke, she surprised me with an immediate request: "Brendon, I want to give my finals speech."

I was shocked. Not understanding her intentions—and, worse yet, forgetting to be encouraging—I said, "Why would you want to give the speech? You do understand you have failed this course, don't you?"

She said, "I know I've messed up. But I've come to class every day because you inspire me, and I knew that if I kept coming you might help me actually get up there in front of the class. I think I'm ready. I want to try this now, Brendon. You've led me this far; please don't lose faith now. I want to do this for you and the class. I have to do this for *me*."

When she said I had inspired her and "led her," something deep inside me felt honored to have helped. I pulled a copy of the speaking schedule out of my binder, put it on the desk, and wrote Sarah's name on the last day of speeches. She stared at her name on the schedule, and when she looked up, she had tears in her eyes. She mumbled thank-you and shuffled out of the office.

We spent the next day talking about what she wanted to accomplish and what I'd like to see her do. It would be a quick two weeks of preparation, but I told her I knew she could do it—without ever having seen her speak publicly before. We met every other day. I spent more than half that time reassuring her that she could do it and coaching her to face her fears. When her faith stumbled, I did my best to pick her up with hope and encouragement. Whenever she ran out of faith, I repeated this quote from Elisabeth Kübler-Ross:

> When you come to the edge of all the light you know and are about to step into the darkness of the unknown, faith is knowing that one of two things will happen: there will be something solid to stand on, or you'll be taught to fly.

I let Sarah know that if her words stumbled, she would find another sentence to stand on, or somehow, in that unbearable moment of uncertainty, she would be given the words to say. She would find her voice simply by *activating* her voice. After two weeks of personally coaching her, I honestly didn't know whether she would show up on her speech day.

But she did. When she approached the podium, nearly half the class turned to me with questioning looks, as if to say, "Is she really going to talk?" Sarah worked her way through ten minutes. During the middle of her speech, she seemed to lose her words for a few seconds—by the expression on her face, a painfully long time for her. She stood there in silence, terrified eyes open like a deer caught in the headlights. I wanted to cheer her on, but no words came out—I was as scared as she was in that moment.

Then one of her classmates encouraged softly, "You've got it, Sarah; it's okay." Her words didn't seem to reach Sarah; she was too detached and transfixed in her own fearful nightmare. But then others started echoing the encouragement. "You can do this Sarah." "Just keep talking, girl; you got this." "Just talk, Sarah; we love you." At this, Sarah finally clicked her eyelids shut once or twice. She looked around the room as if she had just come out of a coma, in disbelief to see all these loving visitors.

More people echoed the encouragement, and in an endearing display of youthfulness, Sarah could be seen repeating their words of encouragement as she locked her eyes on the podium. The audience seemed to be sending a wave of enthusiasm and support toward her, and more than one student teared up. I did, too. And then… she spoke. She lifted her head, smiled, and thanked us, and continued. If I remember correctly, she was supposed to speak for twenty minutes. She sailed on for twice that time. I suppose she hadn't spoken her whole life and had a lot to say!

If I had graded her formally, I imagine she would have gotten a C-minus for content, structure, and presentation. But as she finished, *heart* and heroism won the day, and the class responded with resounding applause as though she had just given the most stirring speech in history. She smiled and walked sheepishly back to her desk. On her way, other students were still clapping, hooting, and giving her praise. A friend glowed and said with great pride, "You *did* it, Sarah." She then stood up and gave Sarah a hug. As Sarah went to sit down, everyone stood up. My class then gave her a standing ovation you would not believe. The feeling in the class was exuberant, and as the class ended, many people walked past Sarah and praised her inspiring performance.

As the last of the class filtered out of the classroom, and I was putting folders in my bag, I caught Sarah out of the corner of my eye, standing alone in the doorway. Turning, I saw tears welling in her eyes. What she said to me next were the most wonderful words I've heard in my life, and reaffirmed to me why we help others. Struggling to hold back tears and the overwhelming emotions she must have felt, Sarah whispered to me as she turned and left, "Thank you, Brendon. No one ever told me my voice was important. You are the only person who has ever told me I had any potential."

Henry David Thoreau wrote: "The mass of men lead lives of quiet desperation." I don't think that desperation is so quiet anymore. If you watch the news, engage in your community, and listen to your loved ones and neighbors, I bet you will hear a thunderous cry for help. People are desperately looking to share their unique voice with the world and to achieve their full potential. They are hungry for new ideas and strategies for improving their personal and professional lives. They are starving for guidance, and they are surprised beyond belief whenever someone offers them a kind word or a helping hand. You can be that surprise for your fellow human beings. That's what this message is all about.

Almost a decade after Sarah walked out of my classroom, I returned to my alma mater to visit a friend. While in town I ran into a few of my former students who happened to be part of that magical day. To my utter amazement and disbelief, not all of them remembered the moment with the level of joy and detail I did. In fact, two barely remembered it at all without my reminding them. Sharing her voice hadn't changed everyone's life, though it had changed mine, and I guarantee it had changed Sarah's. This observation might sound like a downer or a poor way to end the story, but there are very meaningful lessons I hope to convey in sharing this with you.

First, I return to that moment and want to impart this: While it may be scary for you to share your voice with the world, the audience is often more receptive and supportive than you ever imagined.

For Sarah, sharing her voice was terrifying. She had to be coaxed and coached into expressing herself and her ideas publicly. It was a monumental effort for her. But to the rest of the world, it was not a big deal. The audience does not see your preparation, your research, your hard work, or your sweat in getting it right. They just admire and honor the fact that you shared your voice in the first place. Their support and appreciation is almost automatic, because it is human nature to admire the heroic act of self-expression.

You might relate to this. Now that you are armed with all the knowledge I've imparted in this book, the truth is, the final barrier to your sharing your message is fear. When it comes down to it, you may simply be afraid that no one will listen. But they will. Audiences always do. I can tell you with authority that audiences from around the world—whether they are reading you, listening to you, or watching you on video or onstage—have the same desire. They want *value* and when you give them that, they will support you, follow you, buy from you, and honor you. You can take comfort in the fact that almost everywhere in the world, self-expression is seen as an act of art, even heroism. When that act of self-expression is aimed at helping others, then it is viewed as an act of kindness and service. Trust me, people will admire and appreciate you for sharing your voice and your wisdom with others.

Sarah's story also reminds me that no matter how hard we try, we will not always move everyone in our audience. Not everyone who stumbles upon our message will experience a lifelong transformation. Not everyone will get it. Not everyone will remember us years later. But this is only a reiteration of the phrase "When the student is ready the teacher will appear." You will affect those you are meant to. Trust in that.

Although some of my students didn't remember that magical day Sarah spoke, it almost doesn't matter. People have horrible memories anyway, and what's important is that in the moment of her expression, she pulled through, and they did in fact admire and support her. For Sarah, it was a deeply meaningful experience. Imagine that moment in which a shy girl finally set her voice free and then got a standing ovation. It moved me, too, and the entire class that day.

One former student I ran into during my visit to my alma mater *did* remember. She said, "That day taught me that sharing our voice is brave. We can help people if we just speak up and share. I've tried to be brave ever since then." I still remember that day in class as if it were yesterday. I'm still proud of Sarah. I'm still honored to have been part of her story.

I hope that in writing *The Millionaire Messenger* I have become part of *your* story. I hope that you've been inspired to share your own voice and that you continue to do so for life. On your journey to that end, I hope that, like Sarah, your message falls on supportive ears. And I ask that as you see others out there, our fellow messengers in the heroic act of sharing and teaching, that you put your hands together for them. Cheer them on. Tell them their message and their mission is important. We must all celebrate those seeking to serve others with their advice and life experience.

I believe that it's in the act of expressing who you are and what you know that you find yourself. Sharing your voice is important in your ability to grow as a human being, and it's important in your ability to contribute fully to society. Your soul lights up with meaning when you help others take one step more toward their goals. The only question now is whether you will care enough about your growth, contribution, and audience to overcome your fears. You are standing on the world's stage every day and in every moment. Whom will you show up as? Will you sound your voice? What will you say? How will you serve?

Our world is in turmoil and transition. It's in turmoil because we are experiencing such rapid and demanding change in almost every facet of our lives. People around the world are unsure how to cope with the changes they are experiencing in both their personal and professional lives. They don't know what to do, and they don't know where to turn for help. They feel lost amid all the insanity, unsure how to find their place or their potential. Their uncertainty has led to caution and pause that is preventing them from progress. The turmoil is amplified because it seems there are few role models available to help people cope, understand, and get ahead.

We are also experiencing a time of tremendous transition. An entire generation is realizing that there must be more to life than working oneself to an early grave. Tens of millions are being laid off or retiring and looking for new opportunities. Everyone is looking to create more, give more, be involved more, grow more, and connect more. They are exploring their world more readily and, free from the bonds of tradition, are looking for new ideas for achieving their potential. They hunger for guidance and inspiration. Indeed, never before have so many needed ideas and advice for the next stage of their lives, careers, and businesses.

It is in these moments of turmoil and transition that experts shine. We have the opportunity to stand up, share our voice and expertise, and direct others to a greater future for themselves and for all of us. This is our time to lead and serve. Amid all the fear and uncertainty in the world, we can be the light that guides the way.

This is *your* time. Today is the day you choose to be a beacon of hope and help for others: Shine brightly. Share your message. Make a difference.

Talk soon, Expert.

—Brendon

ACKNOWLEDGMENTS

I continue to feel deeply grateful for life's golden ticket—the second chance I was given by God. I live each day to earn that blessing, and in my efforts to live fully, love openly, and make a difference, I am most thankful for His love and guidance.

This book is dedicated to my father, Mel Burchard. We lost you too soon, Dad, but we were so blessed to have you as long as we did. I love you and miss you every day. I will carry your beacon forever: "Be yourself. Be honest. Do your best. Take care of your family. Treat people with respect. Be a good citizen. Follow your dreams."

To Mom, David, Bryan, and Helen—I love you all. I would not be here today without your love, faith, friendship, and support. I'm so proud of you for always being who you are and caring so deeply for our family. You continue to inspire me to be a good man. Mom, you will always be taken care of.

To my sunshine, Denise. You've always believed in me and you've always struggled through with me without hesitation. Can you imagine how far we've come? You still light my world and you are the most kind, impressive person I've ever met. I am in awe of the love we share.

To the group of buddies who've stayed in touch and in my life despite my crazy schedule and poor track record for returning calls or e-mails when I'm on the road. For your lifelong friendship, I love you: Jason Sorenson, Gwenda Houston, Dave Ries, Adam Standiford, Ryan Grepper, Steve Roberts, Jesse Brunner, Matt and Mark Hiesterman, Jeff Buszmann, Jessy Villano Falk, Brian Simonson, Dave Smith, Nick Dedominic, Jenny Owens, Dana Fetrow, Phil Bernard, and Stephan and Mira Blendstrup.

To the first real expert I ever met in my life, my high school journalism teacher, Linda Ballew. If it weren't for you, I would never have developed a love for writing, research, reporting, and spreading important messages within the world. I'm lucky and honored to have been your student.

To my friends and former coworkers at Accenture who taught me about business, excellence, and professionalism, I appreciate you. Thanks especially to Jenny Chan, Mary Bartlett, Teri Babcock, and Janet Hoffman, who helped me follow my own path and find time to write my first novel back in 2004.

Thanks to Scott Hoffman, the best agent in the business. Without you and Roger Freet at HarperOne, *Life's Golden Ticket* would never have seen the shelves, and this wild journey wouldn't have been so fulfilling and successful. You convinced me that a book on my Experts Academy message was my next step, and you were right. Thanks for believing in me.

My story of becoming an expert began by learning from these incredible teachers in the months and years following my car accident at the age of nineteen: Tony Robbins, Paulo Coehlo, James Redfield, Brian Tracy, Stephen Covey, Mark Victor Hansen, Jack Canfield, John Gray, Wayne Dyer, Debbie Ford, Benjamin Hoff, Og Mandino, Marianne Williamson, John Gottman, Nathaniel Branden, Phillip McGraw, Mitch Albom, Les Brown, Deepak Chopra, David Bach, and other legends both living and past. I'm honored to now count many of you as friends and peers. Your voice and wisdom inspired me at a critical life juncture and sowed the seed for this book. I am aware that I stand upon the shoulders of the giants, and I am forever grateful for your guidance and friendship.

Tony Robbins deserves significant credit here for inspiring me to dramatically change the quality of my life following my accident. Before anyone ever called this an industry, he was leading the way. Thanks, Tony, for everything.

In recent years, many of these experts shared invaluable life lessons and marketing ideas, support, or training that helped me spread my message far and wide: Rick Frishman, Steve and Bill Harrison, Jeff Walker, Jim Kwik, Frank Kern, Bill Harris, Srikumar Rao, Eben Pagan, Jay Abraham, Jeff Johnson, Mike Koenigs, Seth Godin, Andy Jenkins, Joe Polish, Ryan Deiss, Tim Ferriss, Yanik Silver, Roger Love, Mike Filsaime, Paul Colligan, Brad Fallon, Garrett Gunderson, Richard Rossi, Trey Smith, Dean Graziosi, Jay Conrad Levinson, David Hancock, Darren Hardy, Daniel Amen, Ken

Kleinberg, Bo Eason, Chris Atwood, Tellman Knudson, Randy Garn, Tony Hsieh, T. Harv Eker, Dean Jackson, Brian Kurtz, Rich Schefren, Brian Johnson, Armand Morin, John Carlton, Vishen Lakhiani, Don Crowther, Jason Van Orden, Jason Deitch, Dan Sullivan, John Assaraf, Paula Abdul. Thanks to you all.

It's impossible to thank everyone who has helped me share my message, so I apologize to all my supporters, affiliates, fans, and friends not listed here. I appreciate you.

Nothing I do today would be possible without a remarkable team. Jenni Robbins, you are the epitome of excellence and the most talented, detailed, efficient, collaborative, and remarkable professional and friend I've ever known. You *are* the Burchard Group. To the rest of the crew who keep me in my place and amplify my works with their brilliance, thank you: Denise McIntyre, Kristy Guthrie, Travis Shields, Shawn Royster, John Josepho, Mel Abraham, Roberto Secades, Tom Dewar. Thanks, too, to our countless and incredibly dedicated volunteers who enliven our events and inspire our customers.

Finally, to my current and future peers in the expert community—I am honored to be in your ranks. This is an industry of brilliant and compassionate people who inspire and instruct others with their advice and knowledge. To all: You are doing important work. Never give up.

ABOUT THE AUTHOR

Brendon Burchard is the founder of Experts Academy and the best-selling author of *Life's Golden Ticket*. He is one of the top business and motivational trainers in the world.

Brendon was blessed to receive life's golden ticket—a second chance—after surviving a dramatic car accident in a developing country. Since then, he has dedicated his life to helping others find their voice, live more fully, and follow their dreams. He founded Experts Academy and wrote *The Millionaire Messenger* to teach emerging advice experts how to have more impact, influence, and income while spreading their message and building their businesses.

An influential multimillionaire expert himself, Brendon inspires over two million people a year with his books, newsletters, products, and appearances. He has been on *ABC World News,* NPR, *Oprah and Friends,* and onstage with the Dalai Lama, Sir Richard Branson, Stephen Covey, Tony Robbins, Deepak Chopra, Marianne Williamson, John Gray, Keith Ferrazzi, T. Harv Eker, Tony Hsieh, David Bach, Jack Canfield, and other leaders and legends in the expert industry. His clients have included the largest companies and nonprofits in the world as well as thousands of executives and entrepreneurs from around the globe who attend his speeches and seminars. Brendon's famous seminars include Experts Academy, High Performance Academy, Partnership Seminar, and World's Greatest Speaker Training.

Meet Brendon and receive free expert training at

www.BrendonBurchard.com.